FIRST 50 SONGS
YOU SHOULD PLAY ON ACOUSTIC GUITAR

ISBN 978-1-4803-9812-2

HAL•LEONARD®
CORPORATION

7777 W. BLUEMOUND RD. P.O. BOX 13819 MILWAUKEE, WI 53213

Visit Hal Leonard Online at
www.halleonard.com

About a Girl

Words and Music by Kurt Cobain

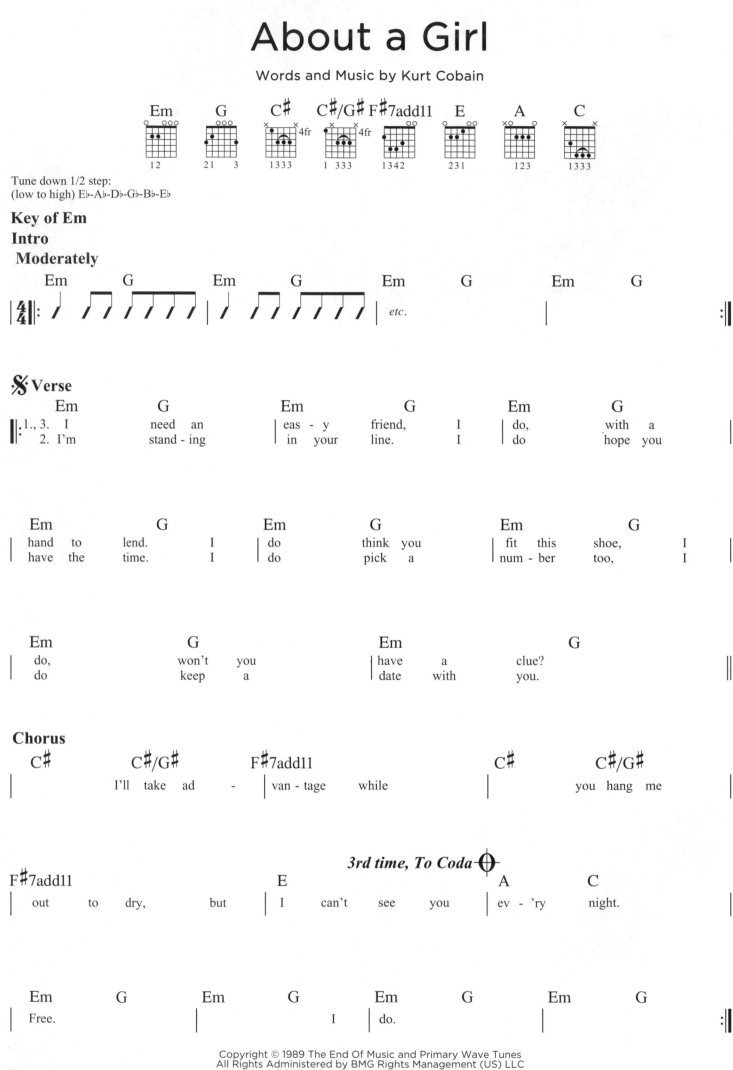

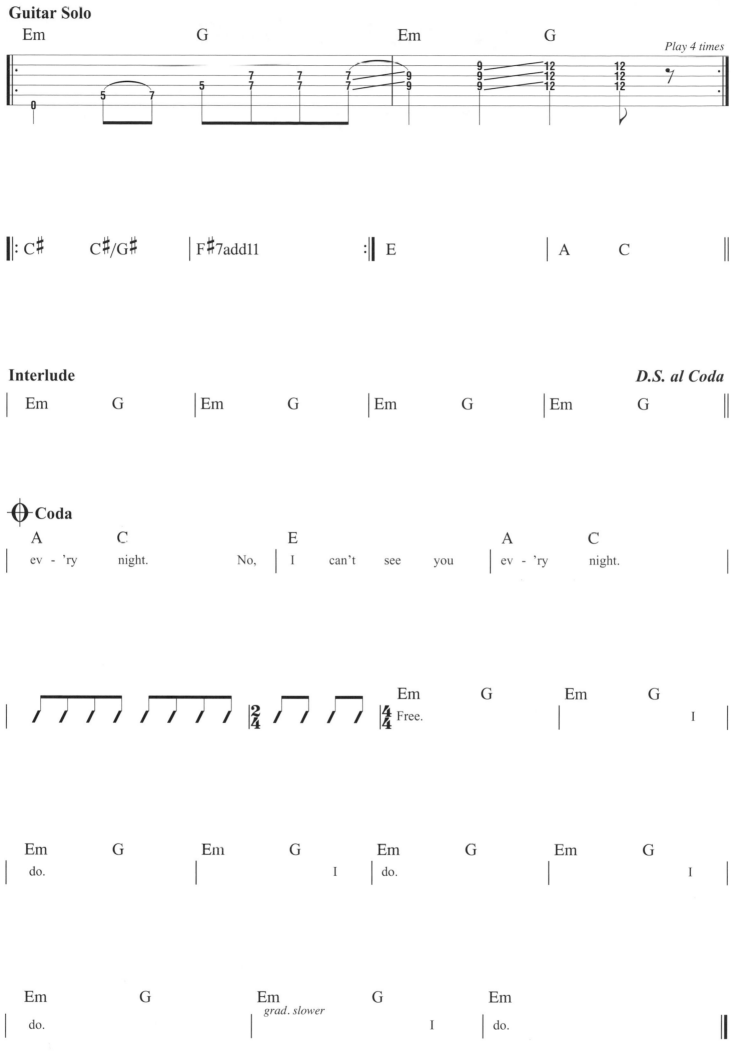

Against the Wind

Words and Music by Bob Seger

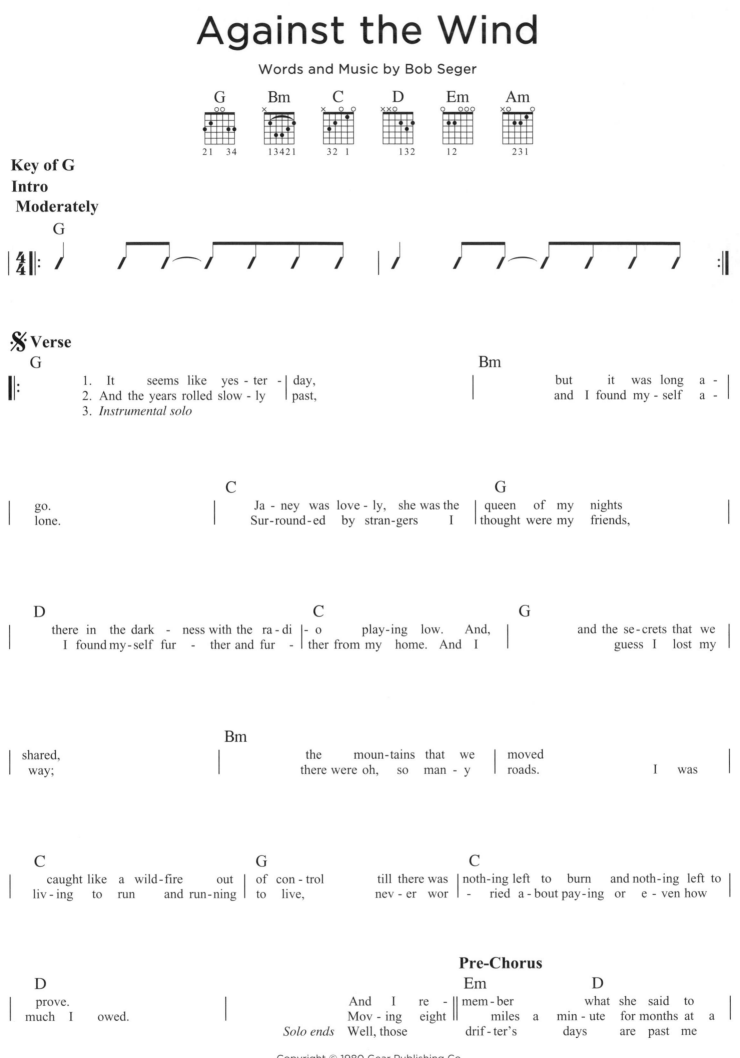

Key of G
Intro
Moderately

.§. **Verse**

G ... Bm

1. It seems like yes-ter-|day, but it was long a-|
2. And the years rolled slow-ly |past, and I found my-self a-|
3. *Instrumental solo*

C ... G

go. Ja-ney was love-ly, she was the |queen of my nights |
lone. Sur-round-ed by stran-gers I |thought were my friends, |

D ... C ... G

there in the dark-ness with the ra-di|-o play-ing low. And, |and the se-crets that we |
I found my-self fur-ther and fur-|ther from my home. And I |guess I lost my |

... Bm

shared, the moun-tains that we |moved |I was |
way; there were oh, so man-y |roads. |

C ... G ... C

caught like a wild-fire out |of con-trol till there was |noth-ing left to burn and noth-ing left to |
liv-ing to run and run-ning |to live, nev-er wor|-ried a-bout pay-ing or e-ven how |

D ... **Pre-Chorus** Em ... D

prove. And I re-|mem-ber what she said to |
much I owed. Mov-ing eight |miles a min-ute for months at a |
Solo ends Well, those drif-ter's days are past me |

4

G		**Em**	**C**		**G**	

me,	how she swore	that it nev - er would end.		I re -
time,	break - ing all	of the rules that would bend,		
now.	I've got so	much more to think a - bout,		

Em		**D**	**C**	

mem - ber how she held me oh,	so tight.	Wish I did-n't know now what I
I be-gan to find my-self search	- ing,	search - ing for shel - ter a - gain
dead-lines and com - mit-ments,		what to leave in,

Chorus

D	**G**	**Bm**

did-n't know then.	A - gainst the wind,	
and a - gain	a - gainst the wind,	
what to leave out.	A - gainst the wind,	

C	**G**	**C**

we were run - nin' a - gainst the wind.	We were young and strong,
lit - tle some-thing a - gainst the wind.	I found my - self seek - ing
I'm still run - nin' a - gainst the wind.	I'm old - er now but still

3rd time, To Coda ⊕   *2nd time, D.S. al Coda*

Am	**C**	**G**

run- nin' a - gainst the wind.		
shel - ter a - gainst the wind.		
run- nin' a - gainst the wind.		

⊕ **Coda**

	C	**Bm**	**D**	

Well, I'm old - er now and still run - nin'	a - gainst the

C	**G**

wind.	(A - gainst the wind.)	(A - gainst the

Outro   *Repeat and fade*

w/ Lead Voc. ad lib.

C	**G**

wind,	a - gainst the wind.)	(A - gainst the

Barely Breathing

Words and Music by Duncan Sheik

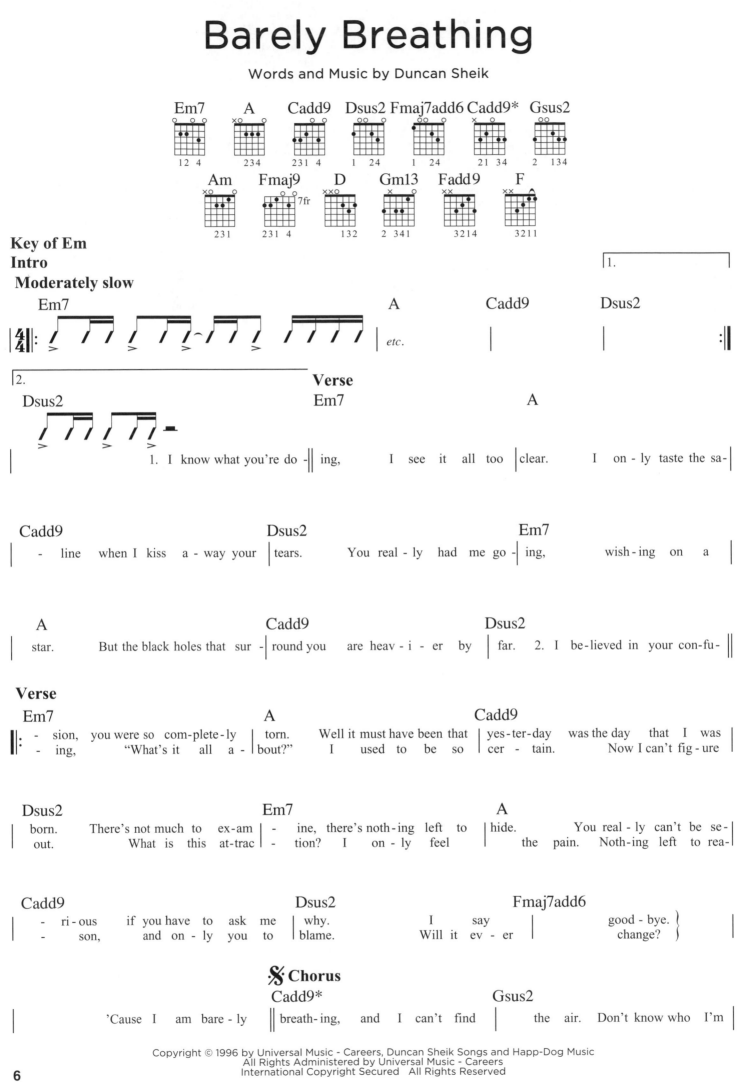

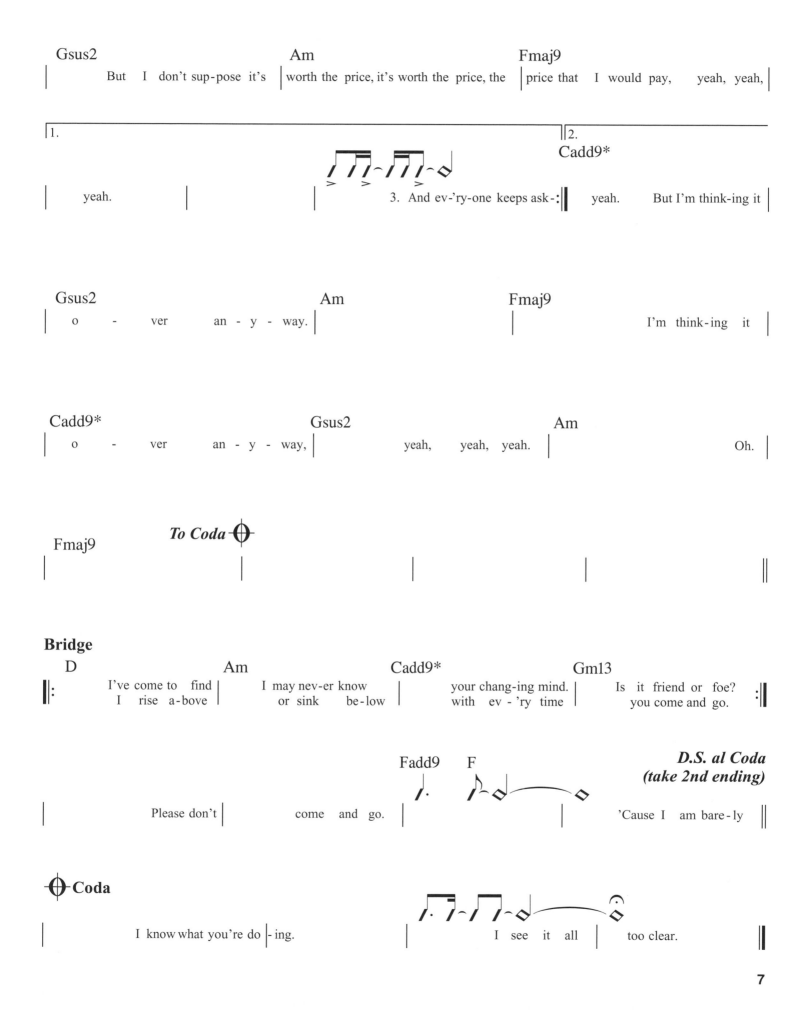

Boulevard of Broken Dreams

Words by Billie Joe
Music by Green Day

Em   G5   D   A   B5   C5

G5*   D5   E5   A/C#   D#5

Capo I

Key of Fm (Capo Key of Em)

Verse

Moderately slow

Em   G5   D   A

$\frac{4}{4}$ 1. I walk a lone - ly road, the | on - ly one that I have ev - er |
2. I'm walk - ing down the line | that di - vides me some - where in my |

Em   G5   D   A

| known. Don't know where it goes, | but it's home to me and I walk a - |
| mind. On the bor - der - line | of the edge and where I walk a - |

Em   G5   D   A

| lone. | | |
| lone. | | |

Em   G5   D   A

| I walk this emp - ty street | on the bou - le - vard of bro - ken |
| Read be - tween the lines of | what's fucked up and ev - 'ry - thing's al - |

Em   G5   D   A   Em   G5

| dreams, where the cit - y sleeps and | I'm the on - ly one and I walk a - | lone. } |
| right. Check my vi - tal signs and | know I'm still a - live and I walk a - | lone. } |

D   A   Em   G5   D   A   B5

| I walk a - lone, I walk a - | lone. | | I walk a - lone, I walk a... ||

Chorus

C5   G5*   D5   E5   C5   G5*

| My shad - ow's the | on - ly one that walks be - side me. | My shal - low heart's |

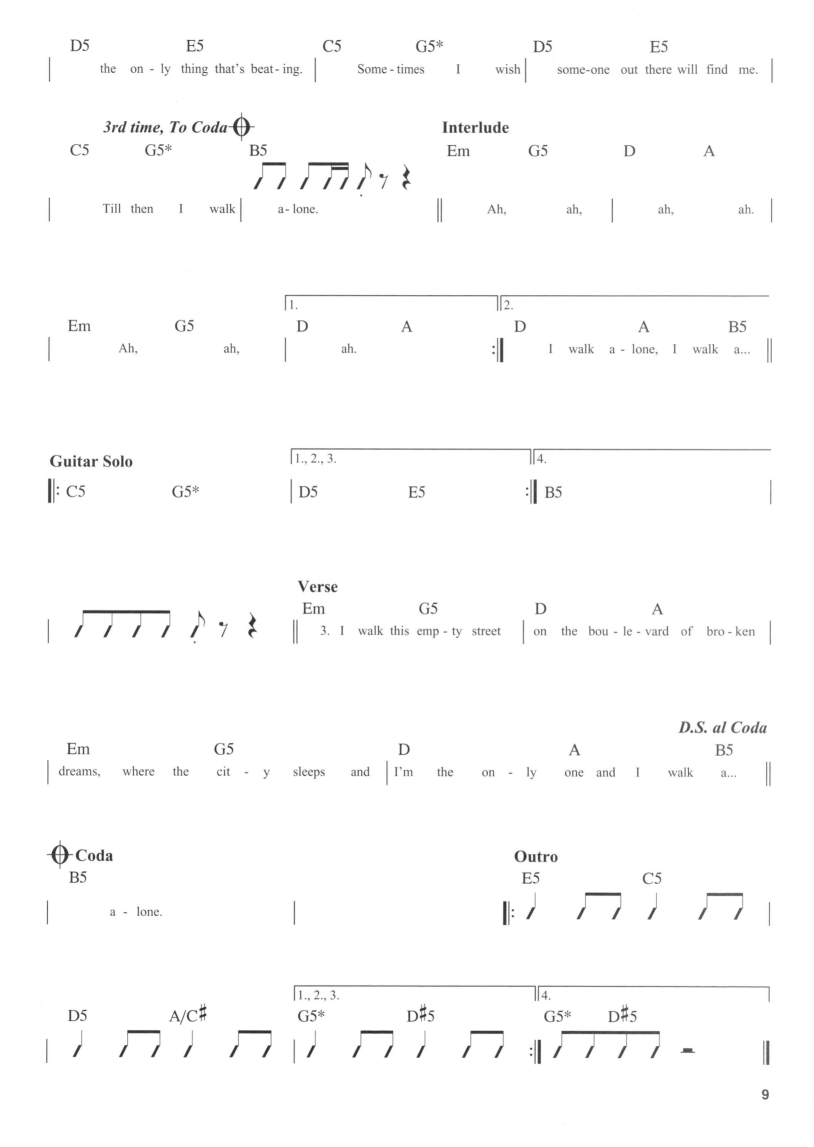

Breaking the Girl

Words and Music by Anthony Kiedis, Flea, John Frusciante and Chad Smith

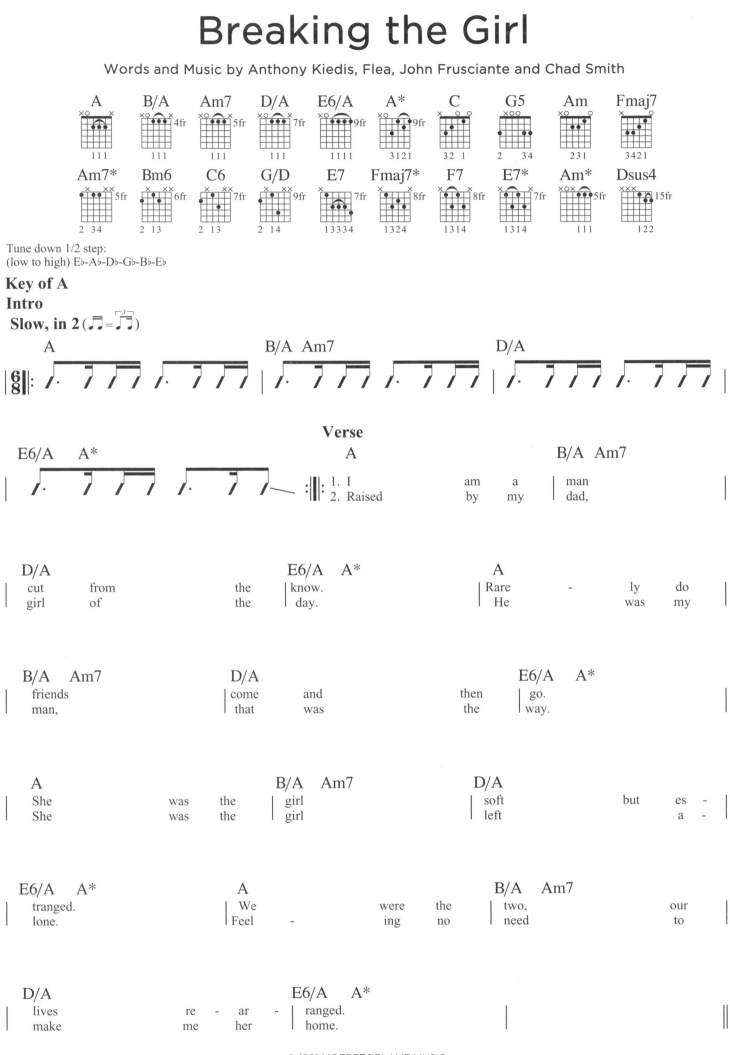

Tune down 1/2 step:
(low to high) Eb-Ab-Db-Gb-Bb-Eb

Key of A
Intro
  Slow, in 2

Pre-Chorus

C		G5		Am	

Feel - ing   so   good   that   day.
I   don't know   what,   when   or   why

C		G5		Fmaj7	

A   feel - ing   of   love   that   day.
the   twi - light   of   love   had   ar - rived.

𝄋 Chorus

Am7*	Bm6	C6	G/D	E7	

Twist - ing   and   turn - ing, your   feel - ings   are   burn - ing, you're   break - ing   the   girl.

Am7*	Bm6	C6	G/D	Fmaj7*	

She   meant   you   no   harm.

Am7*	Bm6	C6	G/D	E7	

Think you're so   clev - er,   but   now   you   must   sev - er, you're   break - ing   the   girl.

3rd time, To Coda ⊕

Am7*	Bm6	C6	G/D	Fmaj7*		F7	E7*	:‖

He   loves   no   one   else.

Interlude

8th time, D.S. al Coda

Am*   * Dsus4   *Play 8 times*

‖: / ⅃ ⅃ ⅃ / ⅃ ⅃ / ⅃ ⅃ / . / . / . :‖

*Bass plays C.

⊕ Coda

Outro

‖: Am7*	Bm6	C6	G/D	E7		

Repeat and fade

Am7*	Bm6	C6	G/D	Fmaj7*		:‖

Bye Bye Love

Words and Music by Felice Bryant and Boudleaux Bryant

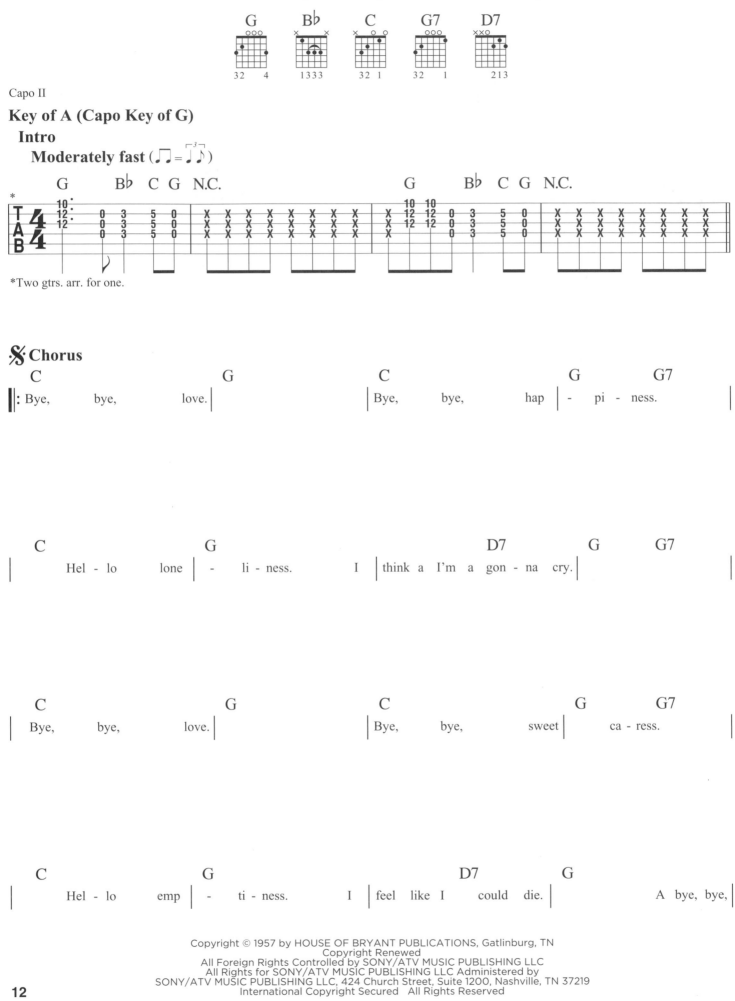

Capo II

Key of A (Capo Key of G)

Intro

Moderately fast

*Two gtrs. arr. for one.

𝄋 Chorus

|: Bye, bye, love. | Bye, bye, hap - pi - ness. |

Hel - lo lone - li - ness. I think a I'm a gon - na cry. |

Bye, bye, love. | Bye, bye, sweet ca - ress. |

Hel - lo emp - ti - ness. I feel like I could die. | A bye, bye, |

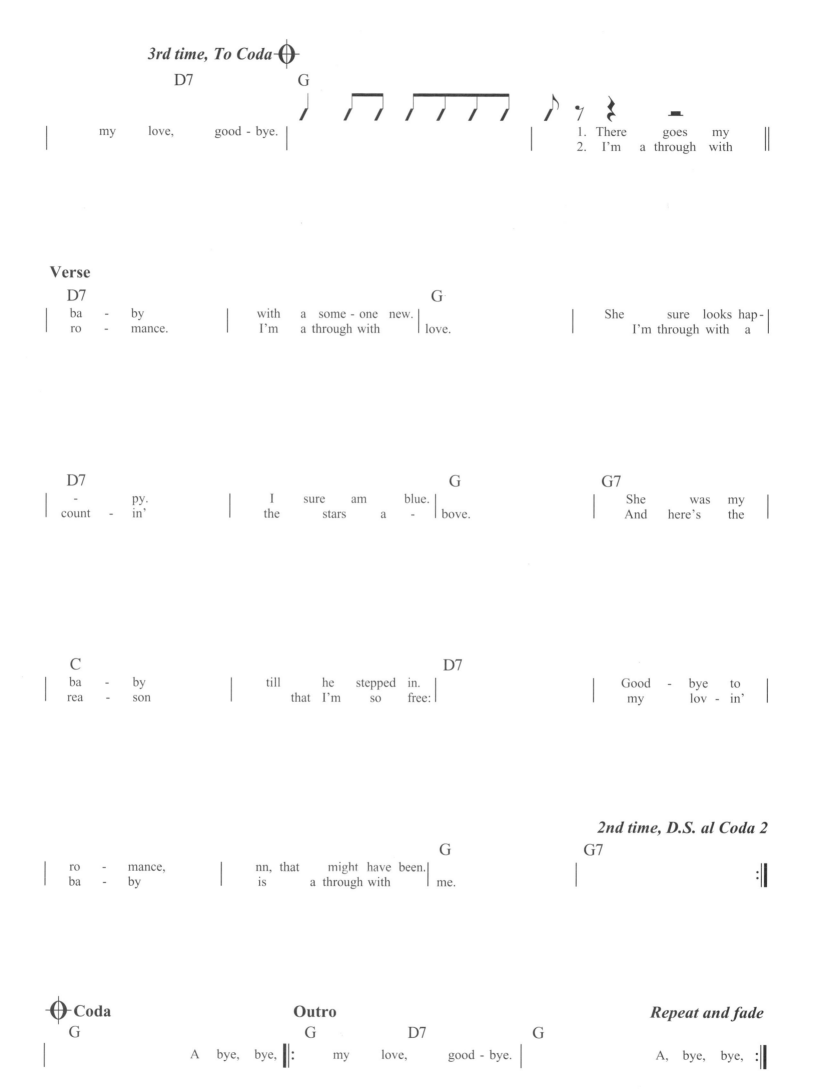

13

Champagne Supernova

Words and Music by Noel Gallagher

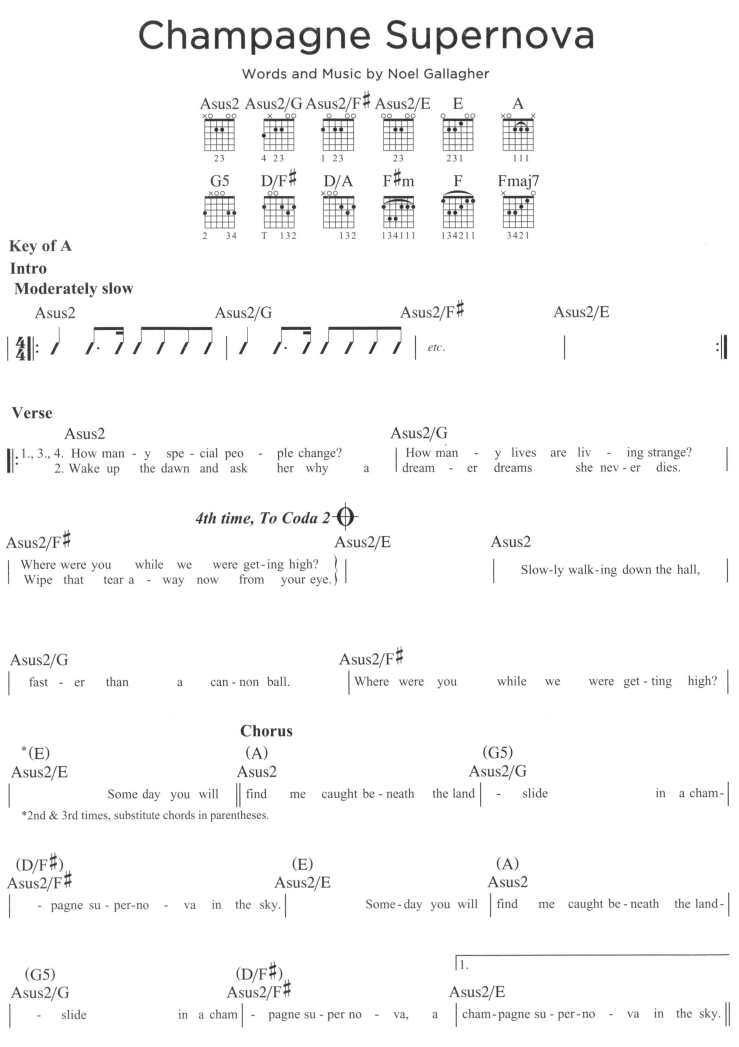

Interlude

| Asus2 | Asus2/G | Asus2/F♯ | Asus2/E :||

2., 3.

Bridge

E   G5

| cham-pagne su-per-no - va. 'Cos || peo-ple be - lieve   that they're | gon-na get a-way for the sum-

A   G5

| - mer. | But | you and I,   we live and die.   The |

2nd time, To Coda 1 ⊕   ***D.C. al Coda 1***
                                                 (take repeat)

D/A   E

| world's still spin-ning 'round, we don't know why, | | why,   why,   why,   why. ||

⊕ **Coda 1**   **Guitar Solo**

                                    A   G5

| why,   why,   why,   why. ||: A | G5 |

D.C. al Coda 2
(take repeat)

Play 4 times

| F♯m | F   G5   :|| F   G5 | F   G5 ||

⊕ **Coda 2**

Asus2/E   Asus2   Asus2/G

| We   were get-ting high. ||:   We   were get-ting high. | We   were get-ting high. |

Outro

Asus2/F♯   Asus2/E   Asus2   Asus2/G

| We were get-ting high. | We were get-ting high. :|| | |

Asus2/F♯   Fmaj7   G5   A
                           grad. slower

| | | | ⌢ ||

Crazy Little Thing Called Love

Words and Music by Freddie Mercury

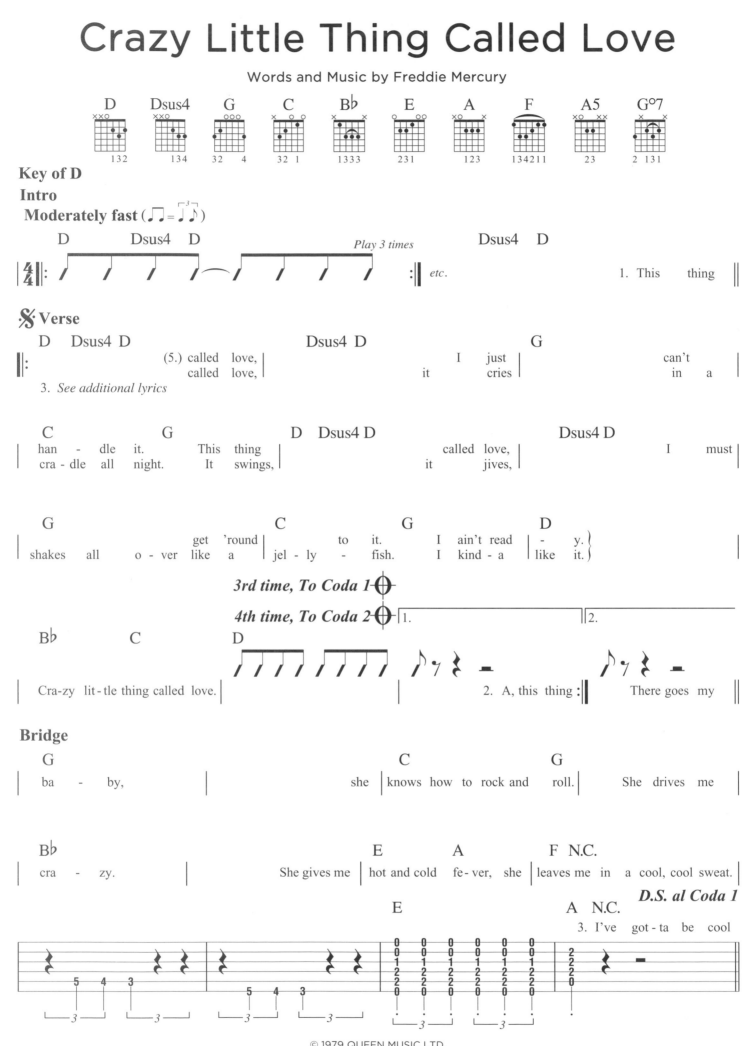

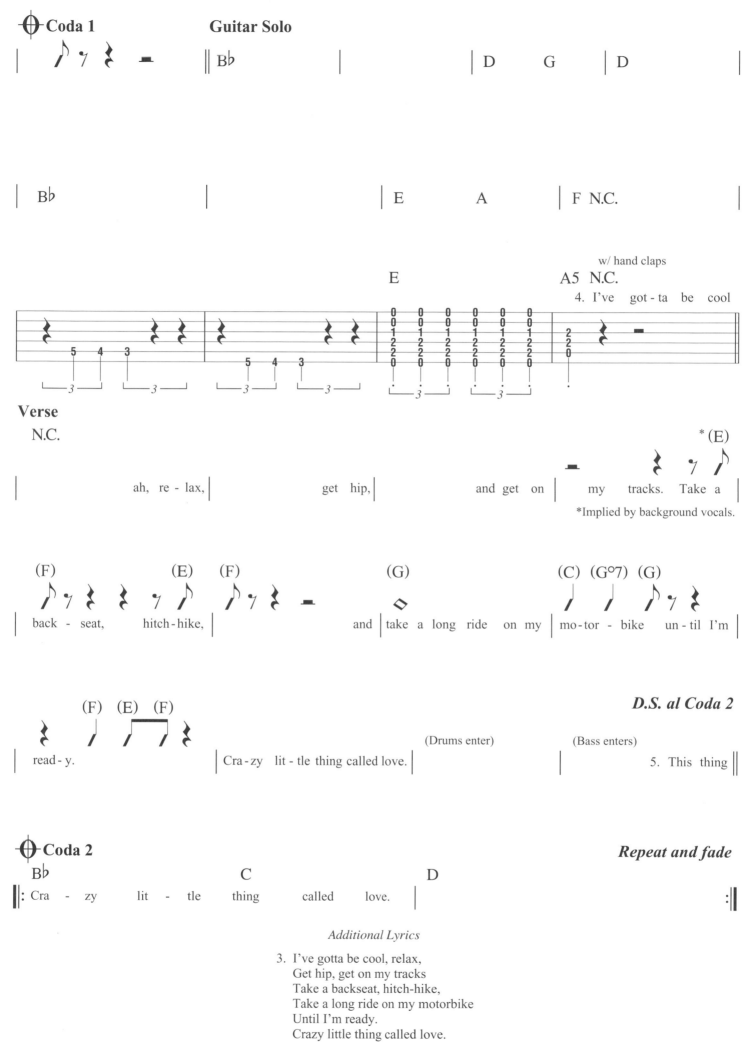

Daughters

Words and Music by John Mayer

Bm7add4   Em7   Em7/A   D   E7   Bm   Em7*

A7sus4   F#m7   Am/D   Gm/D   D*   A13   A7

Bm11   Em7**   Dadd9/F#   Gm9   Dadd4/A   A7(no3rd)   A13(no3rd)

Key of D

Intro

Slow, in 2

Bm7add4   Em7   Em7/A   D

etc.

Verse

Bm7add4   Em7   Em7/A   D

1. I know a | girl; she puts the | col - or in - side of my world. | But |

Bm7add4   Em7   Em7/A   D

she's just like a | maze where all of the | walls all con - tin - ual - ly change. | And |

Bm7add4   Em7   Em7/A   D

I've done all I | can to stand on her | steps with my heart in my hand. | Now |

Bm7add4   Em7   Em7/A   D

I'm start - ing to | see may - be it's got | noth - ing to do with me. |

𝄋 Chorus

Bm7add4   E7   Em7/A   D   Bm7add4   E7   Em7/A   D

Fa - thers, be good to your | daugh - ters. | Daugh-ters will love like you | do. |

3rd time, To Coda 2 ⊕   ***To Coda 1*** ⊕

Bm7add4   E7   Em7/A   D   Bm7add4   E7   Em7/A   D

Girls be-come lov - ers who | turn in - to moth-ers. So | moth-ers, be good to your | daugh - ters, too. |

Interlude

Bm   Em7*   A7sus4   D   Em7* F#m7

| / / / / / / *etc.* | | | / / / / |

Verse

Bm   Em7*   A7sus4   D   Em7* F#m7

| 2. Oh, you see that | skin? It's the | same she's been stand-in' | in since the |

D.S. al Coda 1

Bm   Em7*   A7sus4   D   Em7* F#m7

| day she saw him | walk-ing a-way. Now she's | left clean-ing up the mess he | made. So |

⊕ Coda 1

Bridge

Am/D   Gm/D   D*   A13   A7   Bm11

| Boys, you can | break. You'll | find out how much they can | take. Boys will be |

Em7**   Dadd9/F#   Gm9   A7   Dadd4/A

| strong, and boys sol-dier | on, but boys would be | gone with-out warmth from a | wom - an's |

Interlude

A7(no3rd) A13(no3rd)   Bm7add4   E7   Em7/A   D   Em7/A   D

| good, good heart. ‖: | | :‖ On be-half of |

D.S. al Coda 2

Bm7add4   E7   Em7/A   D   Bm7add4   E7   Em7/A   D

| ev-'ry man look-ing out for | ev-'ry girl, you are the | god and the weight of her | world. So |

⊕ Coda 2

Em7/A   D   Bm7add4   E7   Em7/A   D   Em7/A   D

2nd time, grad. slower

| daugh-ters, too. So ‖: moth-ers, be good to your | daugh-ters, too. So :‖ daugh-ters, too. |

Every Rose Has Its Thorn

Words and Music by Bobby Dall, C.C. Deville, Bret Michaels and Rikki Rockett

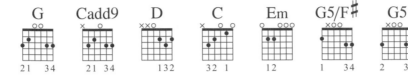

Tune down 1/2 step:
(low to high) E♭-A♭-D♭-G♭-B♭-E♭

Key of G

Intro

Slow

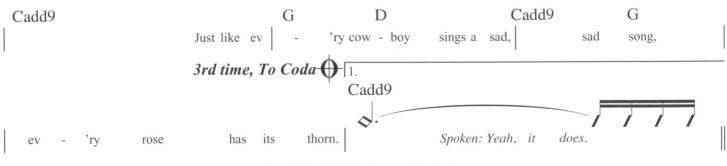

Verse

G Cadd9

1. We both lie si-lent and still in the	dead of the night.	Al-though we
lis-ten to our fav-'rite song play-in' on the	ra-di-o.	Hear the d.
3. I know I could-a saved a love that night if I'd	known what to say.	

G Cadd9

both lie close to-geth-er, we feel	miles a-part in-side.	Was it some-
j. say love's a game of eas-y come and	eas-y go.	But I won-
'Stead of mak-in' love, we both	made our sep-'rate ways.	And now I

G .... Cadd9 .... G Cadd9

- thin' I said or some-thin' I did? Did my words	not come out right?	Though I tried
- der, does he know? Has he ev	- er felt like this?	And I know
hear you found some-bod-y new and	that I nev-er meant that much to you.	To

D C

not to hurt you, though I tried.	But I guess that's why they say
that you'd be here right now if I	could-a let you know some-how. I guess
hear that tears me up in-side and to	see you cuts me like a knife. I guess

Chorus

G .... Cadd9 .... G

| ev-'ry rose has its thorn, | just like ev | - 'ry night has its dawn. |

Cadd9 .... G .... D .... Cadd9 .... G

| Just like ev | - 'ry cow-boy sings a sad, | sad song, |

3rd time, To Coda ⊕ | 1.

Cadd9

| ev-'ry rose has its thorn. | *Spoken: Yeah, it does.* |

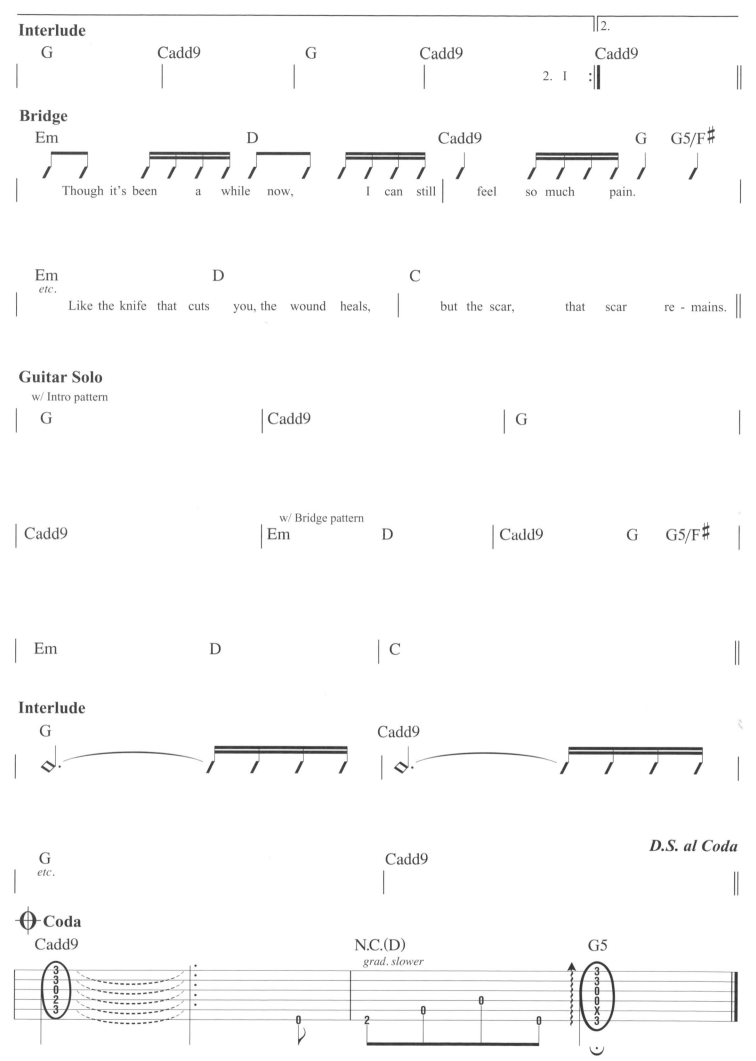

Interlude

G   Cadd9   G   Cadd9   2.   Cadd9

2. I

Bridge

Em   D   Cadd9   G   G5/F#

Though it's been a while now, I can still feel so much pain.

Em   D   C

Like the knife that cuts you, the wound heals, but the scar, that scar re-mains.

Guitar Solo
w/ Intro pattern

G   Cadd9   G

w/ Bridge pattern
Cadd9   Em   D   Cadd9   G   G5/F#

Em   D   C

Interlude

G   Cadd9

D.S. al Coda

G   Cadd9
etc.

⊕ **Coda**

Cadd9   N.C.(D)   G5
grad. slower

Falling Slowly

from the Motion Picture ONCE
from the Broadway Musical ONCE

Words and Music by Glen Hansard and Marketa Irglova

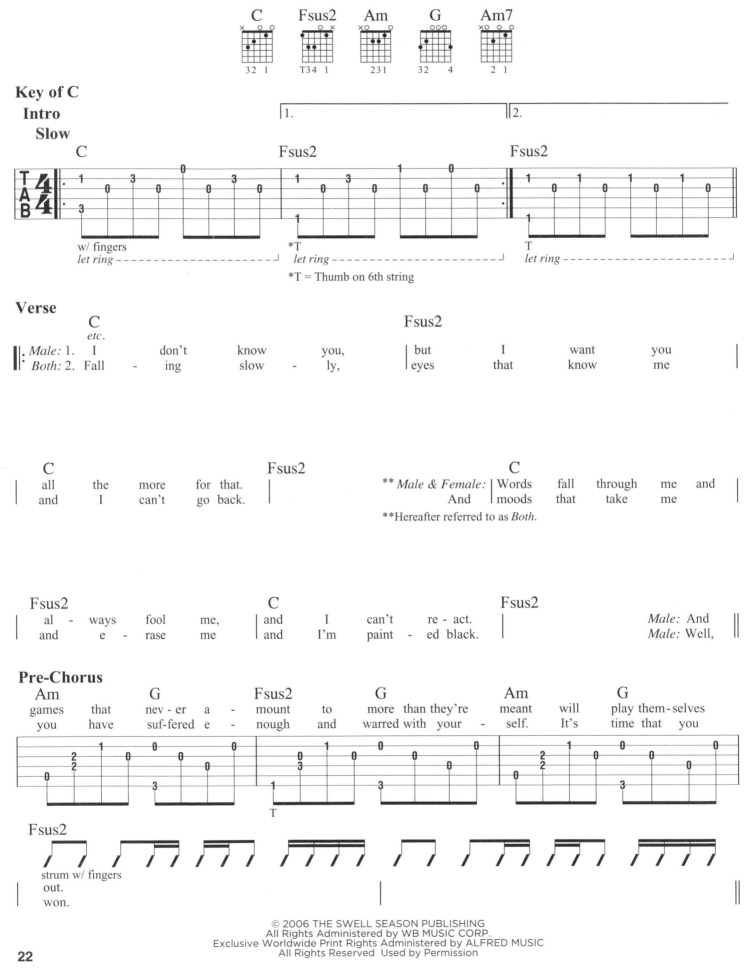

Key of C
Intro
Slow

w/ fingers
let ring

*T
let ring

*T = Thumb on 6th string

T
let ring

Verse

Male: 1. I don't know you, but I want you
Both: 2. Fall - ing slow - ly, eyes that know me

all the more for that.   ** *Male & Female:* Words fall through me and
and I can't go back.   And moods that take me

**Hereafter referred to as Both.

al - ways fool me, and I can't re - act.   *Male:* And
and e - rase me and I'm paint - ed black.   *Male:* Well,

Pre-Chorus

games that nev - er a - mount to more than they're meant will play them - selves
you have suf - fered e - nough and warred with your - self. It's time that you

T

strum w/ fingers
out.
won.

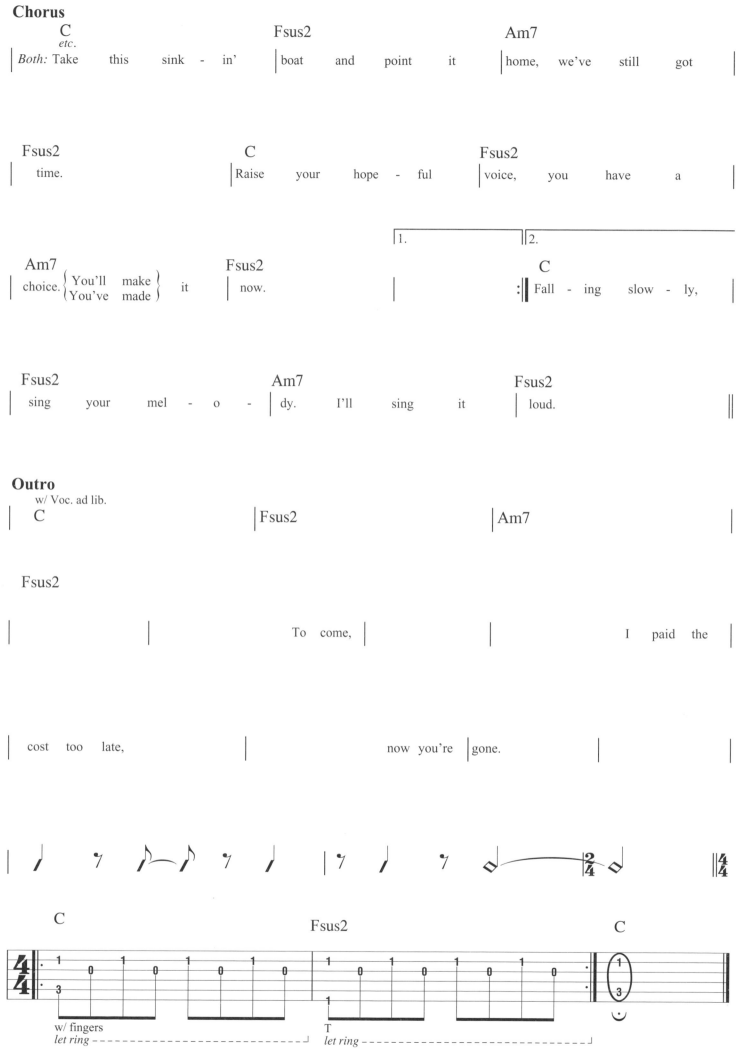

Chorus

C   *etc.*   Fsus2   Am7

Both: Take this sink - in' | boat and point it | home, we've still got |

Fsus2   C   Fsus2

time. | Raise your hope - ful | voice, you have a |

                                                       1.   2.

Am7   Fsus2   C

choice. { You'll make / You've made } it | now. | : | Fall - ing slow - ly, |

Fsus2   Am7   Fsus2

sing your mel - o - | dy. I'll sing it | loud. ‖

Outro

w/ Voc. ad lib.

C | Fsus2 | Am7 |

Fsus2

| | To come, | | I paid the |

| cost too late, | now you're | gone. | |

Fast Car

Words and Music by Tracy Chapman

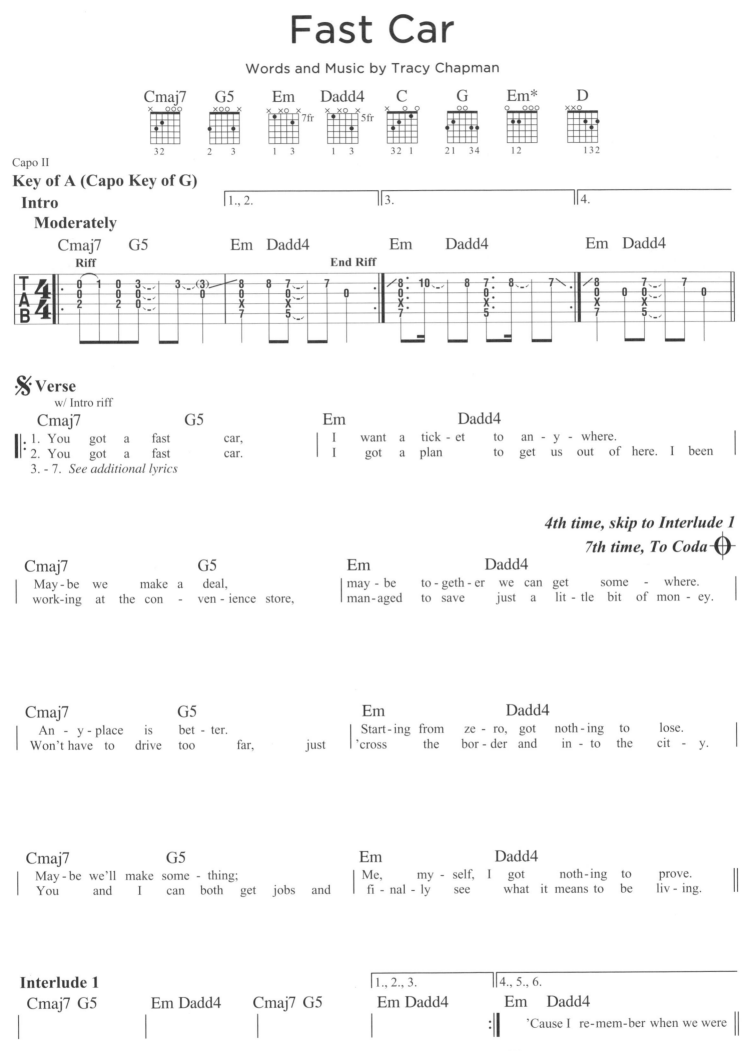

Chorus

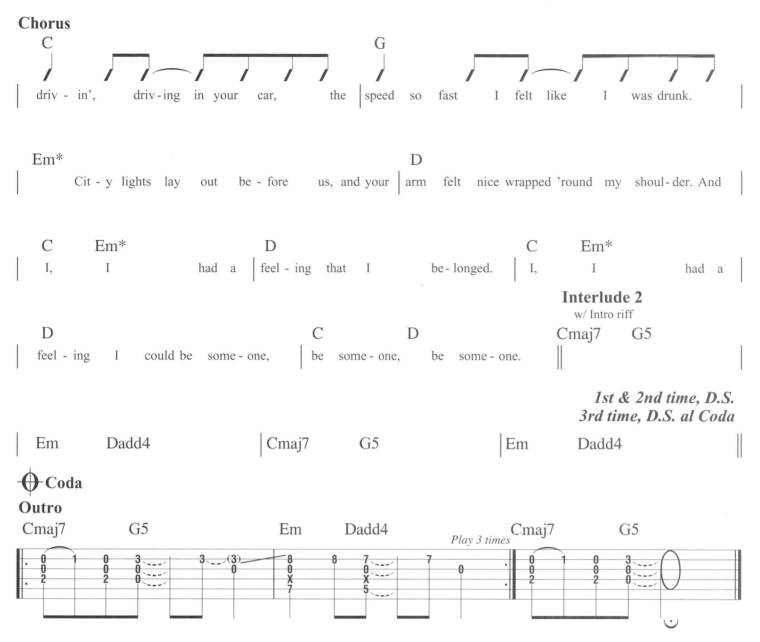

C ... driv-in', driving in your car, the | G speed so fast I felt like I was drunk. |

Em* Cit-y lights lay out be-fore us, and your | D arm felt nice wrapped 'round my shoul-der. And |

C Em* I, I had a | D feel-ing that I be-longed. | C I, Em* I had a |

D feel-ing I could be some-one, | C be some-one, D be some-one. || **Interlude 2** (w/ Intro riff) Cmaj7 G5 |

1st & 2nd time, D.S.
3rd time, D.S. al Coda

| Em Dadd4 | Cmaj7 G5 | Em Dadd4 ||

Coda
Outro

Cmaj7 G5 ... Em Dadd4 ... *Play 3 times* ... Cmaj7 G5

Additional Lyrics

3. You see, my old man's got a problem.
   He live with the bottle, that's the way it is.
   He says his body's too old for working;
   His body's too young to look like his.
   My mama went off and left him;
   She wanted more from life than he could give.
   I said somebody's got to take care of him.
   So I quit school and that's what I did.

4. You got a fast car,
   But is it fast enough so we can fly away?
   We gotta make a decision:
   Leave tonight or live and die this way.
   (To Interlude 1)

5. You got a fast car.
   We go cruising to entertain ourselves.
   You still ain't got a job
   And I work in the market as a checkout girl.
   I know things will get better;
   You'll find work and I'll get promoted.
   We'll move out of the shelter,
   Buy a big house and live in the suburbs.

6. You got a fast car.
   I got a job that pays all our bills.
   You stay out drinking late at the bar,
   See more of your friends than you do of your kids.
   I'd always hoped for better,
   Thought maybe together you and me'd find it.
   I got no plans, I ain't going nowhere,
   So take your fast car and keep on driving.

7. You got a fast car.
   Is it fast enough so you can fly away?
   You gotta make a decision:
   Leave tonight or live and die this way.

Free Fallin'

Words and Music by Tom Petty and Jeff Lynne

E   Asus4/E   Bsus4   E5   A5   B5

Key of E

Intro

Moderately slow

E   Asus2/E   E   Bsus4   E   Asus2/E   E   Bsus4

etc.

1. She's a

Verse

E   Asus2/E   E   Bsus4

good   girl,   loves   her   ma   -   ma,   loves

E Asus2/E   E   Bsus4   E   Asus2/E   E   Bsus4

etc.

Je - sus,   and A - | mer - i - ca,   too.   She's a | good   girl, | cra - zy 'bout   El - vis, loves |

E   Asus2/E   E   Bsus4   E   Asus2/E   E   Bsus4

hors - es   and her | boy- friend,   too. | | 2. And it's a

𝄋 Verse

E   Asus2/E   E   Bsus4

long   day | liv - in'   in   Re - se - da.   There's a |
vam - pires | walk - in' through   the   val - ley   move |
glide   down   o - ver   Mul - hol - land,   I   wan - na |

E   Asus2/E   E   Bsus4

free - way | run - nin' through   the   yard.   And I'm   a |
west   down   Ven - | tu - ra   Bou - le - vard.   And all   the |
write   her   name   in   the   sky.   I'm gon - na |

E   Asus2/E   E   Bsus4

bad   boy   'cause I | don't   e - ven   miss   her.   I'm   a |
bad   boys   are | stand - in'   in   the   shad - ows.   And the |
free   fall   out   in - to   noth - in',   gon - na |

3rd time, To Coda ⊕

E   Asus2/E   E   Bsus4

bad   boy   for | break - in'   her   heart.   And ⎫
good   girls   are | home with   bro - ken   hearts.   Now ⎬ I'm
leave   this   world for   a   while.   Now ⎭

Chorus

E Asus2/E		E Bsus4	E Asus2/E		E Bsus4	
free,		free	ʼfall - inʼ.			Yeah, Iʼm

				1.	**2.**
E Asus2/E		E Bsus4	E Asus2/E	E Bsus4	E Bsus4
free,		free	fall - inʼ.	3. Now all the :‖	

Interlude

E Asus2/E		E Bsus4	E Asus2/E		E Bsus4
			(Free fall - inʼ, Iʼm a		free fall - inʼ, Iʼm a...

D.S. al Coda

E Asus2/E		E Bsus4	E Asus2/E	E Bsus4
			Free fall - inʼ, Iʼm a	free fall - inʼ, Iʼm...) 4. I wan-na

⊕ **Coda**

Chorus

E Asus2/E		E Bsus4	E Asus2/E
free,		free	fall - inʼ.
(Fall - inʼ, Iʼm a	free fall - inʼ, Iʼm a	free	fall - inʼ, Iʼm a

E Bsus4	E Asus2/E	E Bsus4
Yeah, Iʼm	free,	free
free fall - inʼ, Iʼm a...	Fall - inʼ, Iʼm a	free fall - inʼ, Iʼm a

E Asus2/E	E Bsus4	**Interlude** E5 A5
fall - inʼ.		
free fall - inʼ, Iʼm a	free fall - inʼ, Iʼm a...)	

E5 B5	E5 A5	E5 B5
		Yeah, Iʼm
	(Free fall - inʼ, Iʼm a	free fall - inʼ, Iʼm a...)

Outro-Chorus   *Repeat and fade*

E Asus2/E	E Bsus4	E Asus2/E	E Bsus4
free,	free	fall - inʼ.	Oh!
‖: *(Free fall - inʼ, Iʼm a	free fall - inʼ, Iʼm a,	free fall - inʼ, Iʼm a	free fall - inʼ, Iʼm a...) :‖

*Bkgds enter 2nd time.

27

Have You Ever Seen the Rain?

Words and Music by John Fogerty

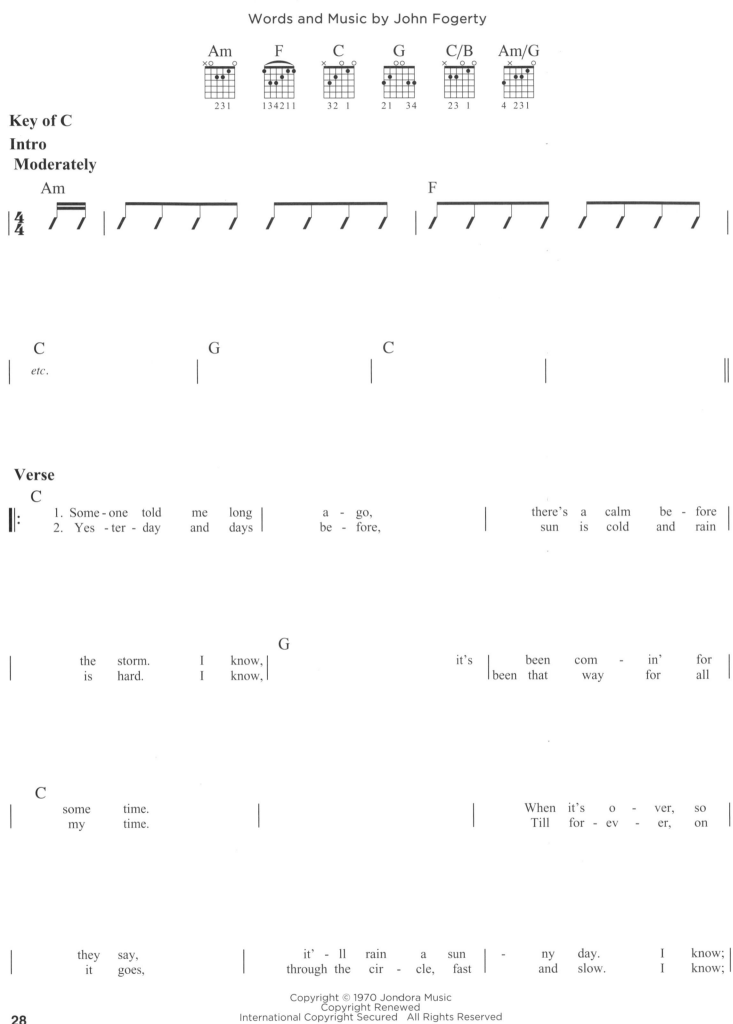

Key of C
Intro
Moderately

Verse

1. Some-one told me long a - go, there's a calm be - fore
2. Yes - ter - day and days be - fore, sun is cold and rain

the storm. I know, it's been com - in' for
is hard. I know, been that way for all

some time. When it's o - ver, so
my time. Till for - ev - er, on

they say, it' - ll rain a sun - ny day. I know;
it goes, through the cir - cle, fast and slow. I know;

G   C

| shin - in' down   like | wa - ter.
| it can't   stop,   I   won | - der.

Chorus

F   G   C   *(C/B)   Am   **(Am/G)

I   want to | know,   have you | ev - er   seen   the | rain?

*Optional: Bass plays B.   **Optional: Bass plays G.

F   G   C   (C/B)   Am   (Am/G)

I   want to | know,   have you | ev - er   seen   the | rain

F   G   C

| 1. | 2.

com - in' down | a sun - ny day? | :||

F   G   C   (C/B)   Am   (Am/G)

I   want to | know,   have you | ev - er   seen   the | rain?

F   G   C   (C/B)   Am   (Am/G)

I   want to | know,   have you | ev - er   seen   the | rain

F   G   C   G   C

com - in' down | a sun - ny day? |

Hey There Delilah

Words and Music by Tom Higgenson

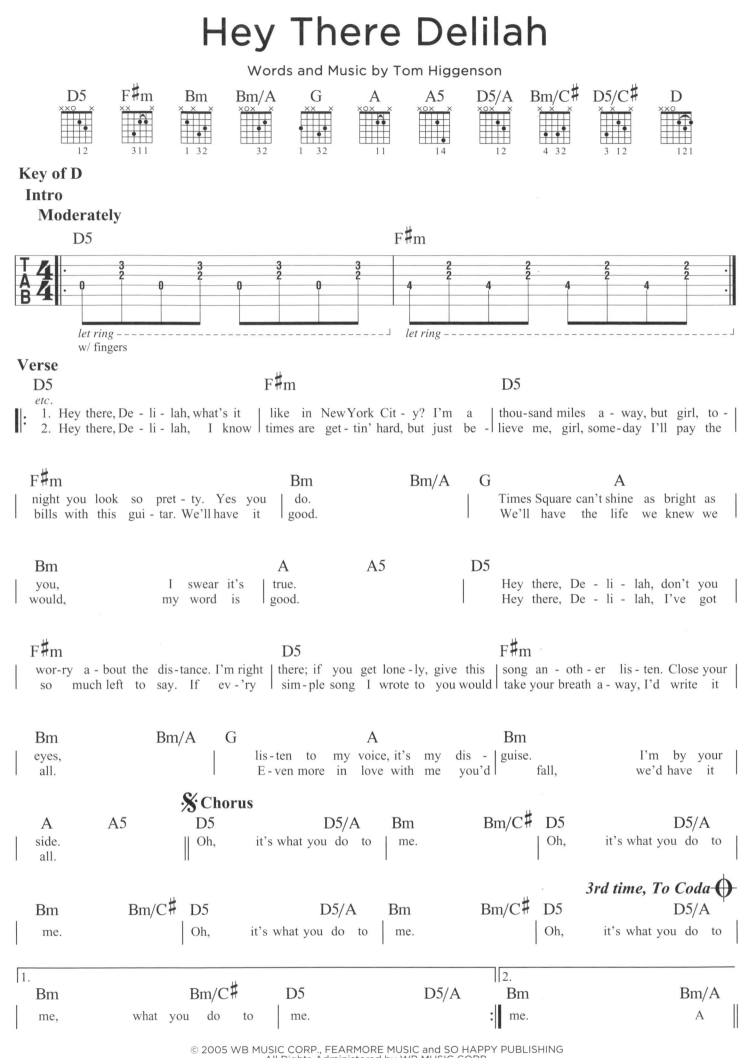

Bridge

G / / A / / D5 / / D5/A
| thou-sand miles seems pret-ty far, but | they've got planes and trains and cars. I'd | walk to you if I had no oth-er |

Bm / / Bm/A / G / / / A
| way. Our | friends would all make fun of us and | we'll just laugh a-long be-cause we |

D5 / / D5/C♯ / Bm / / Bm/A / G
| know that none of them have felt this | way. De -| li - lah, I can prom-ise you that |

A / / / / Bm
| by the time that we get through, the | world will nev - er ev - er be the | same, and you're to |

Verse

A / / A5 / / D5
| blame. | | 3. Hey there, De - li - lah, you be |

F♯m / / / D5 / / F♯m
| good and don't you miss me. Two more | years and you'll be done with school and | I'll be mak-in' his-t'ry like I |

Bm / / Bm/A / G / / / A / / Bm / / Bm/A
| do. | You'll know it's all be - cause of | you. |

G / A / / Bm / / Bm/A / G / / / A
| We can do what-ev - er we want | to. | Hey there, De - li - lah, here's to |

D.S. al Coda

Bm / / / A / / / A5
| you, this one's for | you. | ‖

𝄌 **Coda**   **Outro** | 1. - 4.   ‖ 5.
w/ Voc. ad lib.

Bm / / Bm/C♯ / D5 / / D5/A / Bm / / Bm/C♯ / D
| me, what you do to ‖: me. | | :‖ 𝄌 ‖

31

Ho Hey

Words and Music by Jeremy Fraites and Wesley Schultz

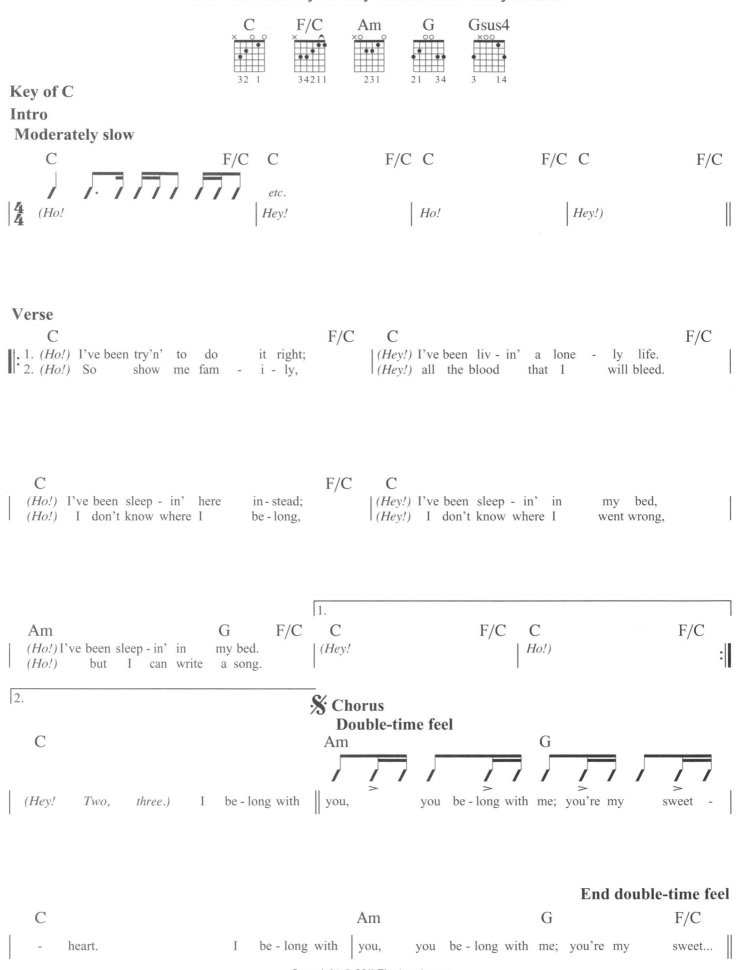

Key of C
Intro
Moderately slow

Verse

Chorus
Double-time feel

End double-time feel

Interlude
w/ Intro pattern

To Coda ⊕

C	F/C C	F/C C	F/C C	F/C
(Ho!	*Hey!*	*Ho!*	*Hey!)*	

Verse

C	F/C C	F/C
3. *(Ho!)* I don't think you're right for him.	*(Hey!)* Look at what it might have been	if you

C	F/C C	Am G F/C
(Ho!) took a bus to Chi - na town.	*(Hey!)* I'd be stand - in' on Ca - nal	*(Ho!)* and Bow - er - y.

C	Am	G F/C C
(Hey!	*Ho!)* And she'd be stand - in' next to me.	*(Hey! Two, three.)* I be - long with

Chorus
Double-time feel
w/ Chorus pattern

|1. |2.

Am	G	C	C	
‖: you, you be-long with me; you're my sweet	- heart.	I be-long with :‖	- heart.	‖

Bridge

F/C	C Gsus4	C	F/C	C Gsus4
Love,	we need it now. Let's hope		for	some. 'Cause

D.S. al Coda   ⊕ **Coda**

F/C	C Gsus4	C	C
oh,	we're bleed - in' out.	I be-long with ‖	*Hey!)* ‖

A Horse with No Name

Words and Music by Dewey Bunnell

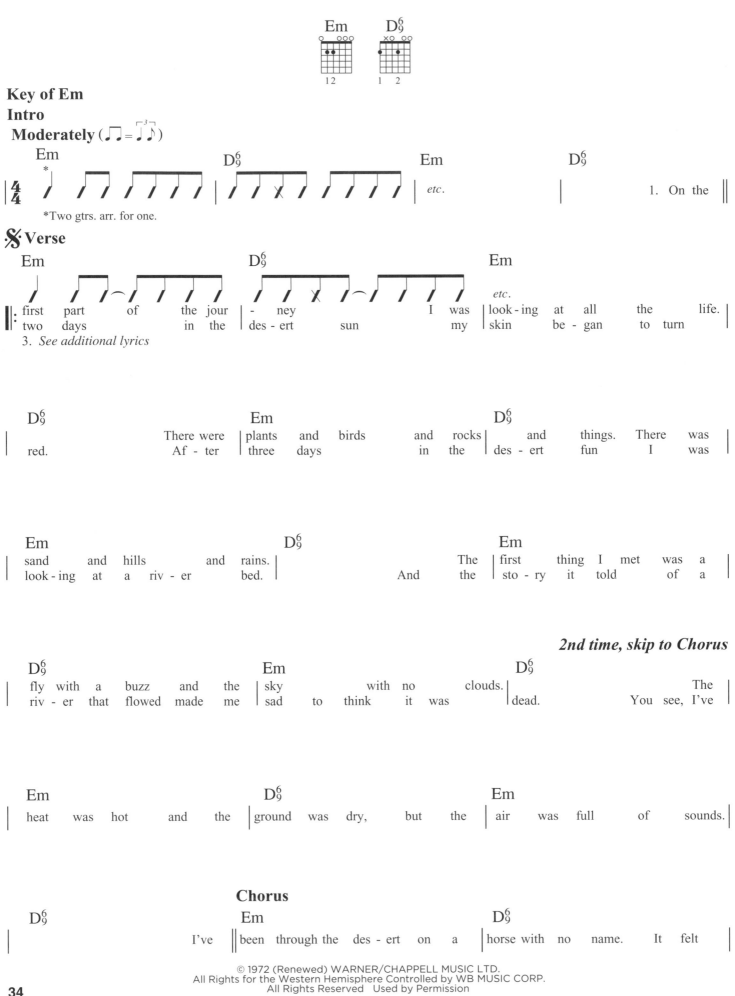

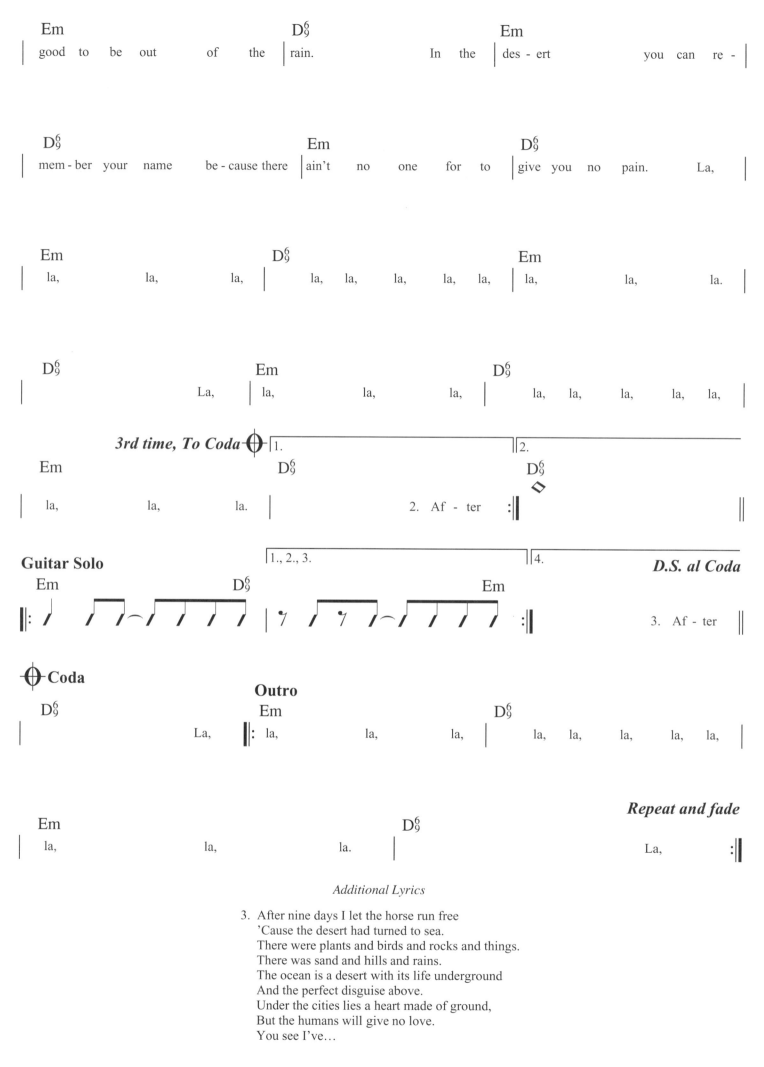

Additional Lyrics

3. After nine days I let the horse run free
   'Cause the desert had turned to sea.
   There were plants and birds and rocks and things.
   There was sand and hills and rains.
   The ocean is a desert with its life underground
   And the perfect disguise above.
   Under the cities lies a heart made of ground,
   But the humans will give no love.
   You see I've…

I Won't Give Up

Words and Music by Jason Mraz and Michael Natter

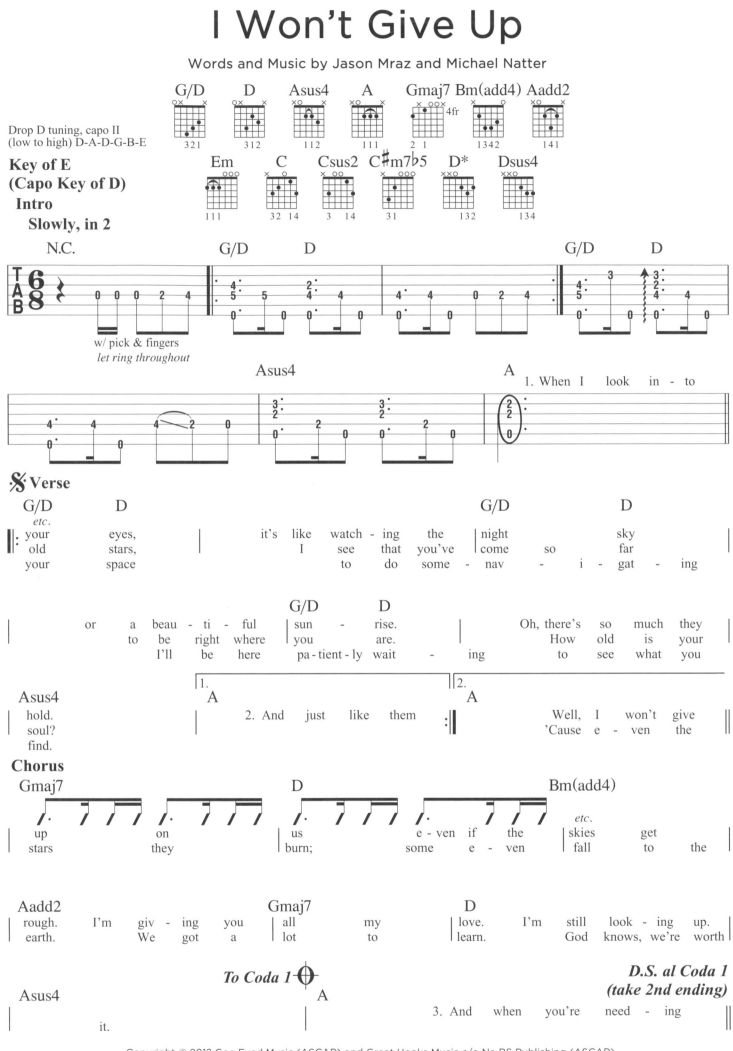

Drop D tuning, capo II
(low to high) D-A-D-G-B-E

Key of E
(Capo Key of D)
Intro
Slowly, in 2

w/ pick & fingers
let ring throughout

1. When I look in-to

Verse

your eyes, it's like watch-ing the night sky
old stars, I see that you've come so far
your space to do some-nav-i-gat-ing

or a beau-ti-ful sun-rise. Oh, there's so much they
to be right where you are. How old is your
I'll be here pa-tient-ly wait-ing to see what you

1.
hold. 2. And just like them
soul?
find.

2.
Well, I won't give
'Cause e-ven the

Chorus

up on they
stars burn;

us, e-ven if the skies get
some e-ven fall to the

rough. I'm giv-ing you all my love. I'm still look-ing up.
earth. We got a lot to learn. God knows, we're worth

To Coda 1 ⊕

D.S. al Coda 1
(take 2nd ending)

it.
3. And when you're need-ing

⊕ Coda 1

A   Gmaj7

| No,   I   won't   give   up. | | I   don't ‖

Bridge

Em

‖: wan - na   be   some-one   who   walks   a - way   so   eas - i - | ly. I'm here   to   stay   and make the   dif - fer - ence that |
    dif - f'renc - es,   they   do   a   lot   to teach us how to | use the tools and gifts we got; yeah,   we got   a |

┌1.   ┌2.

A   Asus4   A   Asus4   A

| I   can   make. | Our :‖   And   in   the |
| lot   at   stake. |

C   Csus2   C   Csus2

| end, you're still   my friend; at   least we   did   in - tend   for | us   to   work. We   did - n't break; we   did - n't burn. |

C#m7♭5

| We had to learn   how to bend | with - out the world   cav - ing in. | C   Csus2   I   had to learn   what I   got |

C#m7♭5   N.C.   D*   Dsus4   D*

| and   what   I'm   not   and   who   I | am. | I   won't   give ‖

𝄋𝄋 Chorus

Gmaj7   D   Bm(add4)   Aadd2

‖: (3.) up   on | us   e - ven   if   the | skies   get | rough. I'm   giv - ing   you |
     up   on | us.   God   knows, I'm | tough   e - | nough.   We've   got   a |

3rd time, To Coda 2 ⊕ ┌1.

Gmaj7   D   Bm(add4)

| all   my | love.   I'm   still   look - ing   up. | I'm   still   look - ing   up. |
| lot   to | learn.   God   knows, we're   worth |

┌2.   *D.S.S. al Coda 2*   ⊕ Coda 2

Aadd2   Asus4   A   Asus4

| Well, I   won't   give :‖   it. | I   won't   give ‖ | 𝄽. ‖

Into the Mystic

Words and Music by Van Morrison

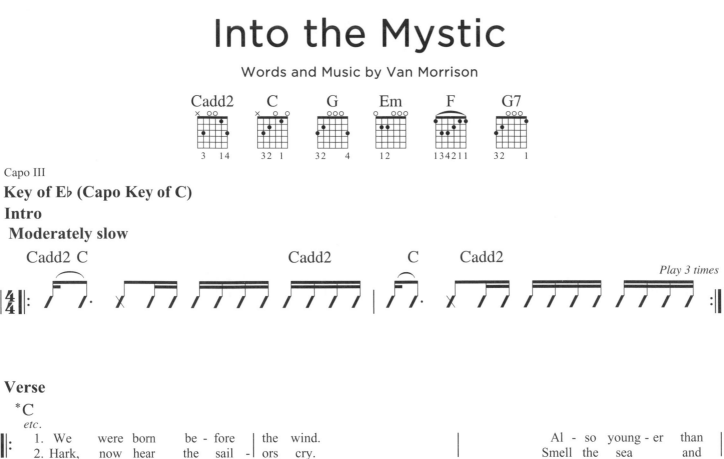

Capo III

Key of E♭ (Capo Key of C)
Intro
Moderately slow

Cadd2 C   Cadd2   C   Cadd2

Play 3 times

Verse

*C
etc.

1. We   were born   be - fore | the wind. | Al - so young - er than
2. Hark, now hear   the sail - | ors   cry. | Smell the sea   and

*Chord symbols reflect basic harmony.

                                        G
the sun. | Ere the bon - nie boat was | won   as we sailed in - to the
        feel the sky. | Let your   soul | and spir - it fly   in - to the

                                                        |1.   ‖2.
C
mys - tic. | :‖ |
mys - tic. | ‖

Pre-Chorus

2nd time, w/ Lead voc. ad lib.

Em   F   C
‖:   And when that fog horn | blows   I | will be com - in' home. |

                Em   F
| Yeah, when the fog horn | blows   I   wan - na |

G   **G7**

| hear   it, | I   don't   have   to   fear   it   and   I ‖

Chorus

C

| wan - na   rock   your | gyp - sy   soul | just   like   way   back |

                                         G

| in the days of old. | { And mag - nif - i-cent - | ly we will float   in - to   the |
| { And   to - geth-er we will | flow   in - to   the |

C
| mys -   tic. |
| mys -   tic. | C' - mon   girl. ‖

Instrumental

| **C** | | | |

| **G** | | **C** | ⌐1.   :‖

⌐2.   **G**   **C**

| Too late   to   stop   now. | | | ‖

Layla

Words and Music by Eric Clapton and Jim Gordon

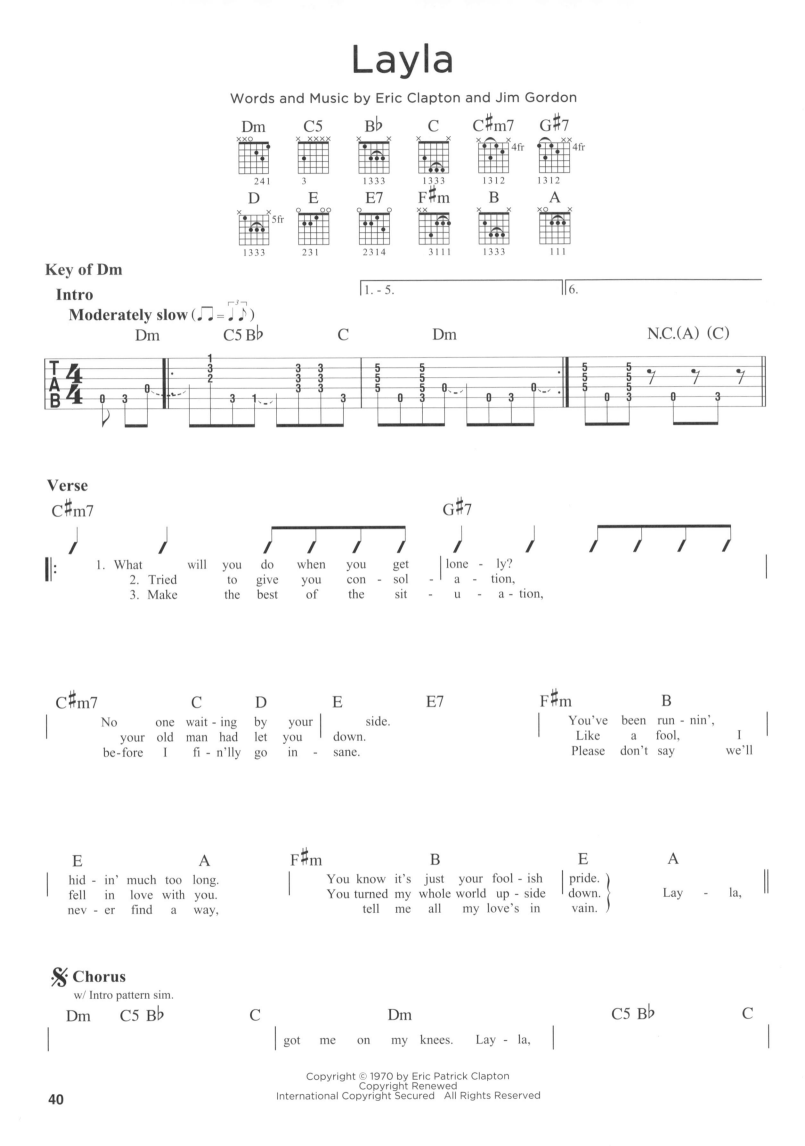

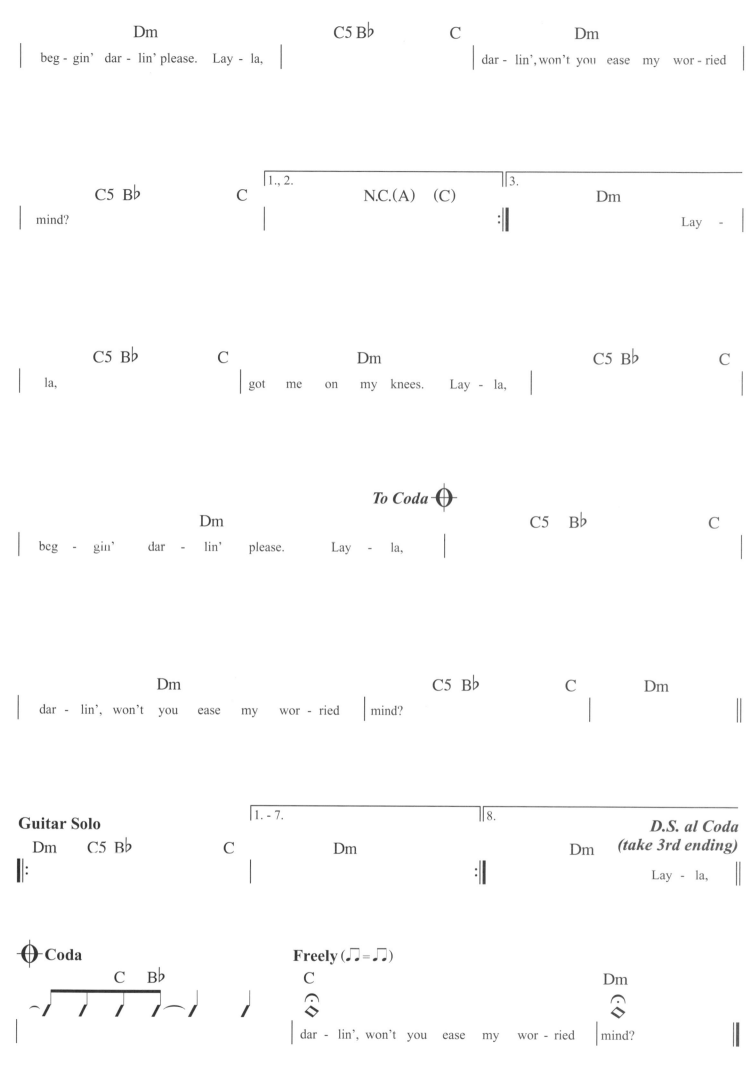

Let Her Go

Words and Music by Michael David Rosenberg

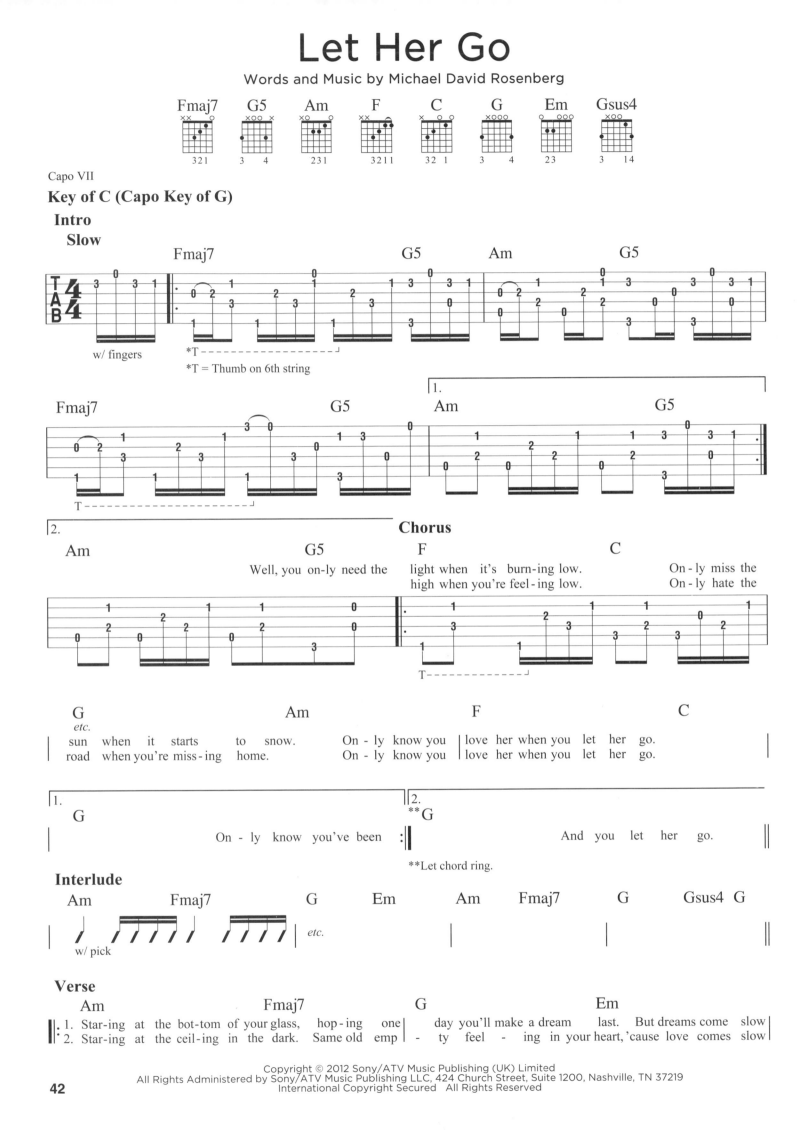

Am		Fmaj7		G		Gsus4	G	

and   they   go   so   fast.
and   it   goes   so   fast.   You
                                                                                 Well,   you

Am		Fmaj7		G		Em		

see her when you close   your eyes.   May-be   one   day you'll un-der-stand why   ev -'ry-thing you
see her when you fall   a - sleep.   But nev - er   to touch   and   nev-er   to keep 'cause you loved her too

Am		Fmaj7		G		Gsus4		G

touch   sure - ly   dies.
much   and   you dived   too   deep.   But
                                                                      Well,   you   on - ly   need   the

𝄋 Chorus

*Fmaj7		C		G		Am		

light when it's burn-ing low.   On - ly miss the   sun when it starts to   snow.   On - ly know you

*4th time, let chords ring.

Fmaj7		C	G	**Gsus4	G	

love her when you let her go.   On - ly know you've been

**4th time, N.C. till end.

Fmaj7		C		G		Am		

high when you're feel-ing low.   On - ly hate the   road when you're miss-ing home.   On - ly know you

3rd time, To Coda 1 ⊕

4th time, To Coda 2 ⊕

1.						2.		

| Fmaj7 | | C | G | Gsus4 | G | | G | Gsus4 | G |

love her when you let her go.   :‖   And you let her go,

Bridge

Am		Fmaj7		G		Gsus4	G	Am		Fmaj7	

oh,   oh,   oh, | no.   And you let her go, | oh,   oh,   oh,

G		Gsus4		G	Am		Fmaj7		G	Em	

no.   Well, you let her go.

D.S. al Coda 1

Am	Fmaj7		G		Gsus4		G

                              'Cause   you   on - ly   need   the

⊕ **Coda 1**   *D.S. al Coda 2*   ⊕ **Coda 2**

G		Gsus4		G

'Cause you on - ly need the ‖   And you let her go.

43

Malagueña

from the Spanish Suite ANDALUCIA
Music and Spanish Lyric by Ernesto Lecuona
English Lyric by Marian Banks

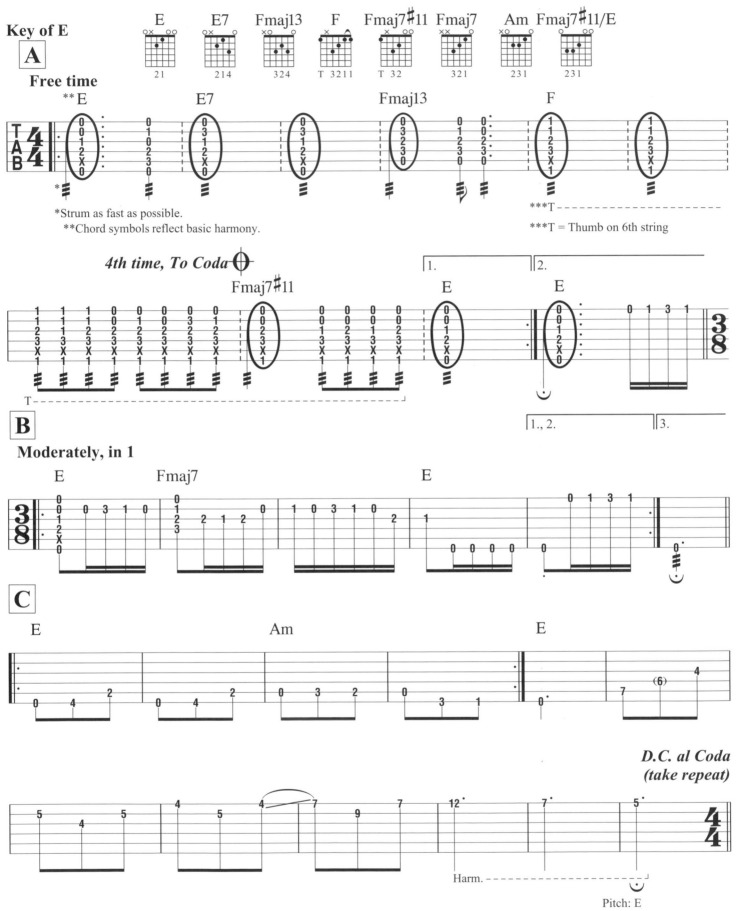

*Strum as fast as possible.
**Chord symbols reflect basic harmony.

***T = Thumb on 6th string

D.C. al Coda
(take repeat)

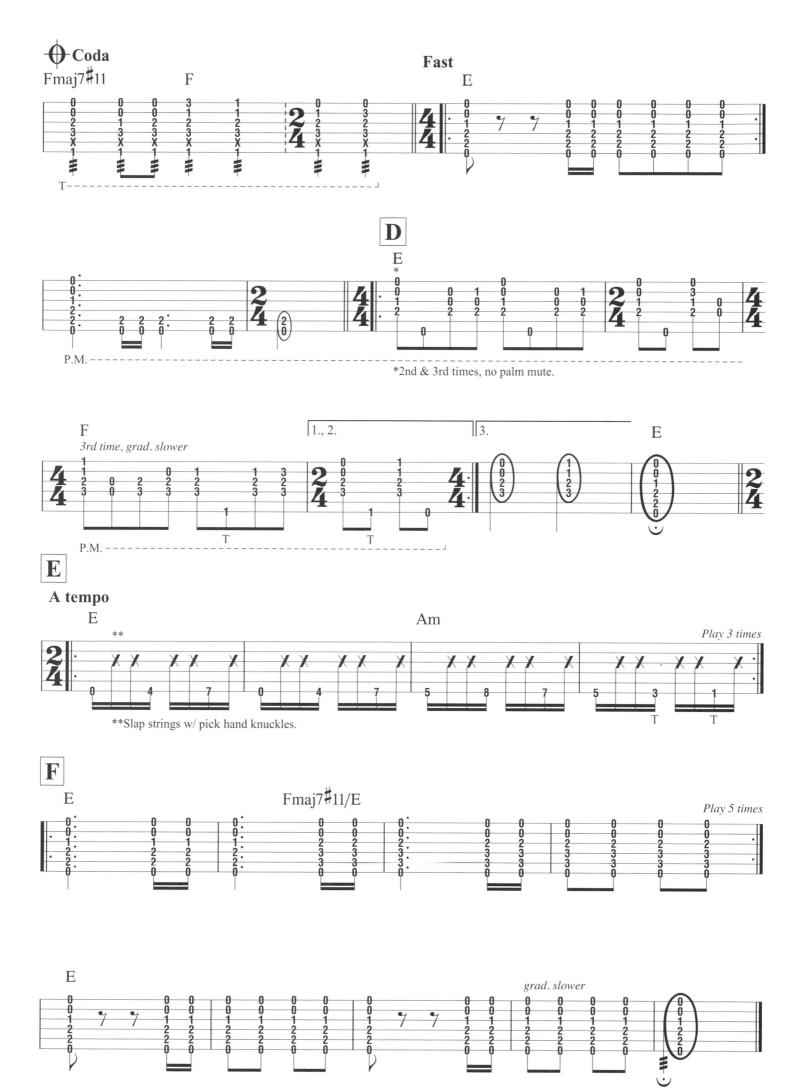

Me and Julio Down by the Schoolyard

Words and Music by Paul Simon

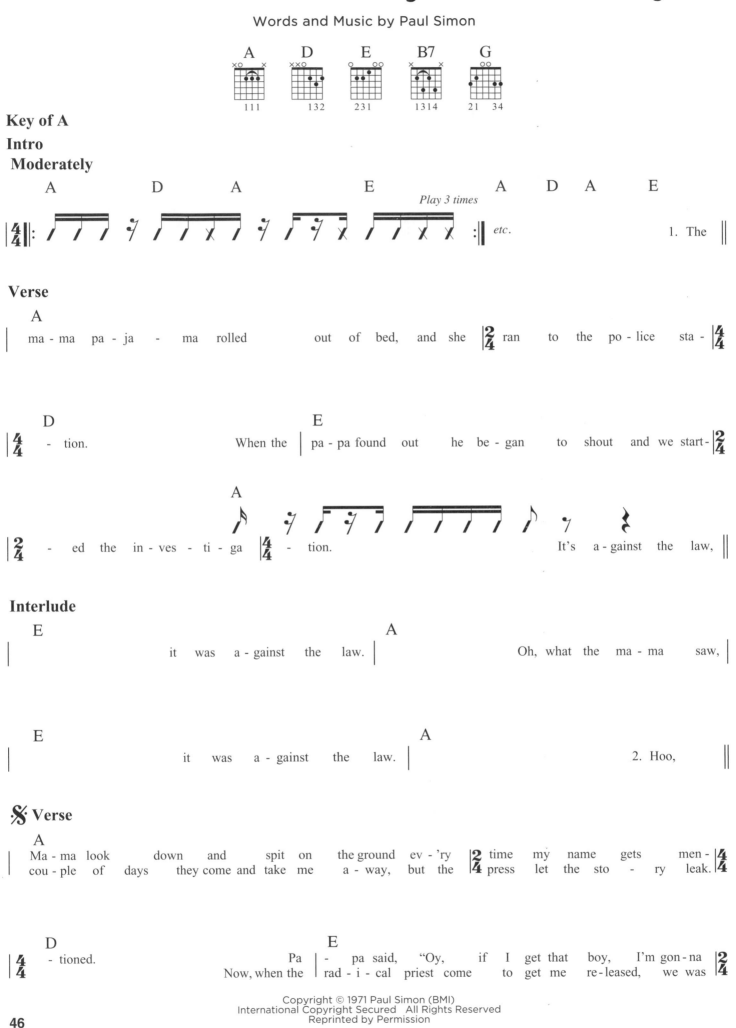

Key of A

Intro

Moderately

Play 3 times

1. The

Verse

ma - ma pa - ja - ma rolled out of bed, and she ran to the po - lice sta -

- tion. When the pa - pa found out he be - gan to shout and we start-

- ed the in - ves - ti - ga - tion. It's a - gainst the law,

Interlude

it was a - gainst the law. Oh, what the ma - ma saw,

it was a - gainst the law. 2. Hoo,

Verse

Ma - ma look down and spit on the ground ev - 'ry time my name gets men -
cou - ple of days they come and take me a - way, but the press let the sto - ry leak.

- tioned. Pa - pa said, "Oy, if I get that boy, I'm gon - na
Now, when the rad - i - cal priest come to get me re - leased, we was

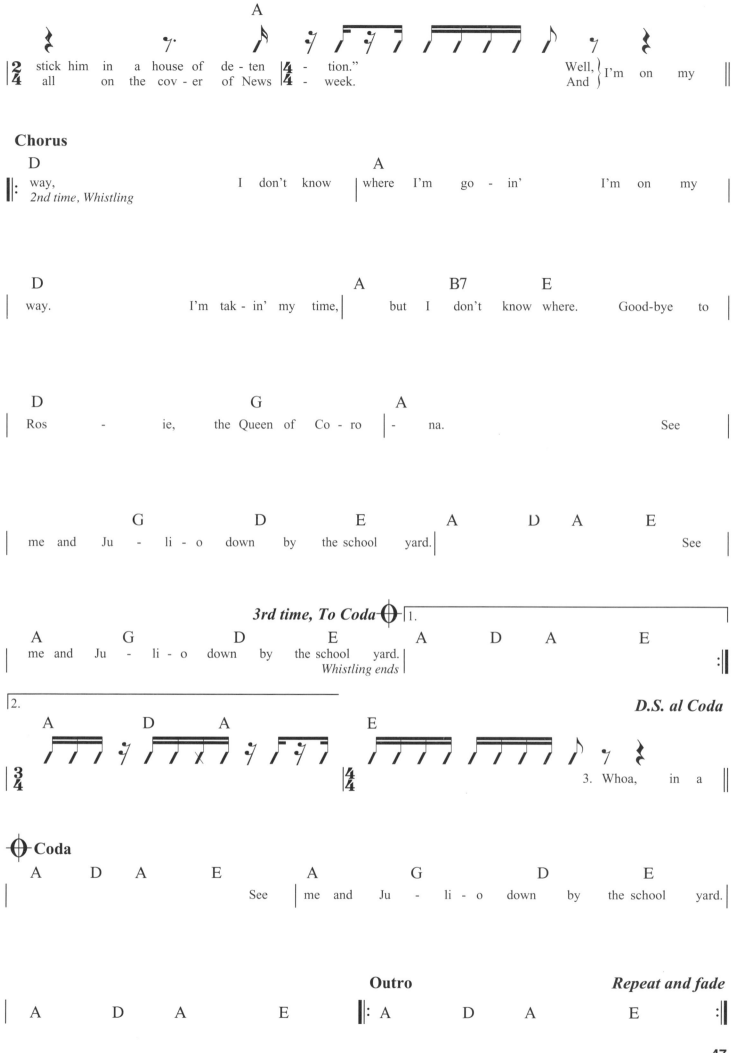

Mean

Words and Music by Taylor Swift

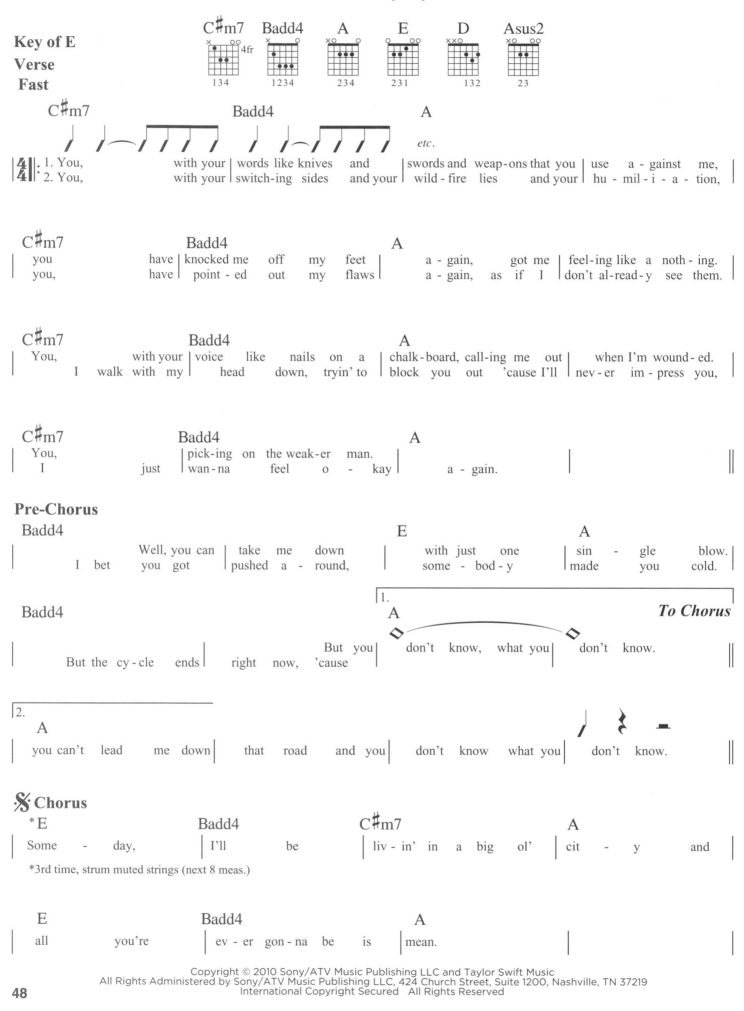

Key of E
Verse
Fast

C#m7   Badd4   A   E   D   Asus2

C#m7   Badd4   A

etc.

4/4
1. You,   with your | words like knives   and | swords and weap-ons that you | use   a - gainst   me, |
2. You,   with your | switch-ing sides   and your | wild - fire lies   and your | hu - mil - i - a - tion, |

C#m7   Badd4   A

| you   have | knocked me   off   my   feet | a - gain,   got me | feel-ing like a noth - ing. |
| you,   have | point - ed   out   my   flaws | a - gain, as if I | don't al - read - y   see them. |

C#m7   Badd4   A

| You,   with your | voice like nails on a | chalk-board, call-ing me out | when I'm wound - ed. |
| I walk with my | head   down, tryin' to | block you out 'cause I'll | nev - er im - press you, |

C#m7   Badd4   A

| You, | pick-ing on the weak-er man. |
| I   just | wan - na feel o - kay | a - gain. |

Pre-Chorus

Badd4   E   A

| Well, you can | take me   down | with just   one | sin - gle   blow. |
| I bet   you got | pushed a - round, | some - bod - y | made   you   cold. |

Badd4   1.   A   ***To Chorus***

| But you | don't   know, what you | don't know. |
| But the cy - cle ends | right now, 'cause |

2. A

| you can't   lead   me down | that road   and you | don't know what you | don't know. |

𝄊 Chorus

*E   Badd4   C#m7   A

| Some - day, | I'll   be | liv - in' in a big ol' | cit - y   and |

*3rd time, strum muted strings (next 8 meas.)

E   Badd4   A

| all   you're | ev - er gon - na be is | mean. |

E		Badd4		C#m7		A	
Some -	day,	I'll	be	big e-nough so you can't		hit me and	

3rd time, To Coda 1 ⊕   *4th time, To Coda 2* ⊕

E		Badd4		A			
all	you're	ev - er gon - na be is	mean.			Why you got - ta be so	

Interlude

E				D E		1.	2. Badd4
mean?							

Mandolin Solo

Asus2		Badd4	Asus2		
				And I can	

Bridge

Badd4			E		A	
see you years from now	in a bar,	talk-ing o - ver a	foot - ball game,
with that same big	loud o-pin - ion but	no - bod-y's	lis - ten - ing.

Badd4		C#m7	Badd4
Washed up and rant	- ing a - bout the	same old	bit - ter

Asus2		Badd4	
things.		Drunk and grum - blin' on	a - bout how

C#m7	Badd4	Asus2	
I	can't	sing.	But all you are is

Interlude

E		Badd4		C#m7		A	
mean.						All you are is	

E		Badd4		C#m7	
mean	and a	li - ar	and pa -	thet - ic	and a -
mean,	and	mean,	and	mean,	and

2nd time, D.S. al Coda 1   ⊕ Coda 1   *D.S. al Coda 2*   ⊕ Coda 2

A			E	
lone in life and		Why you got - ta be so...		mean?
mean. But...				

Melissa

Words and Music by Gregg Allman and Steve Alaimo

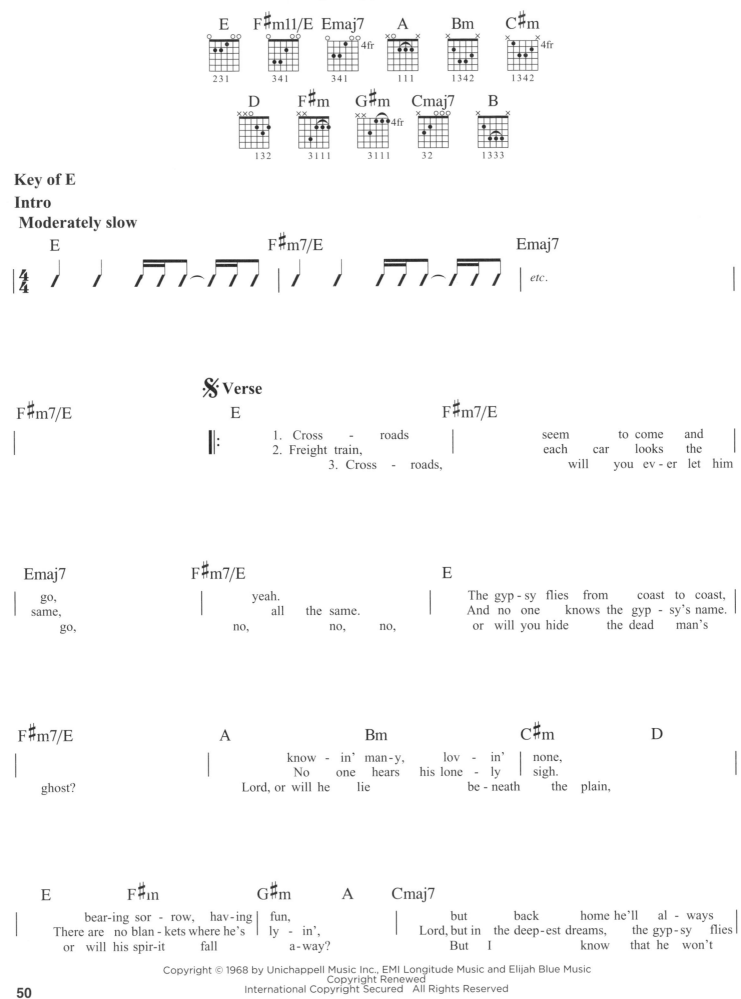

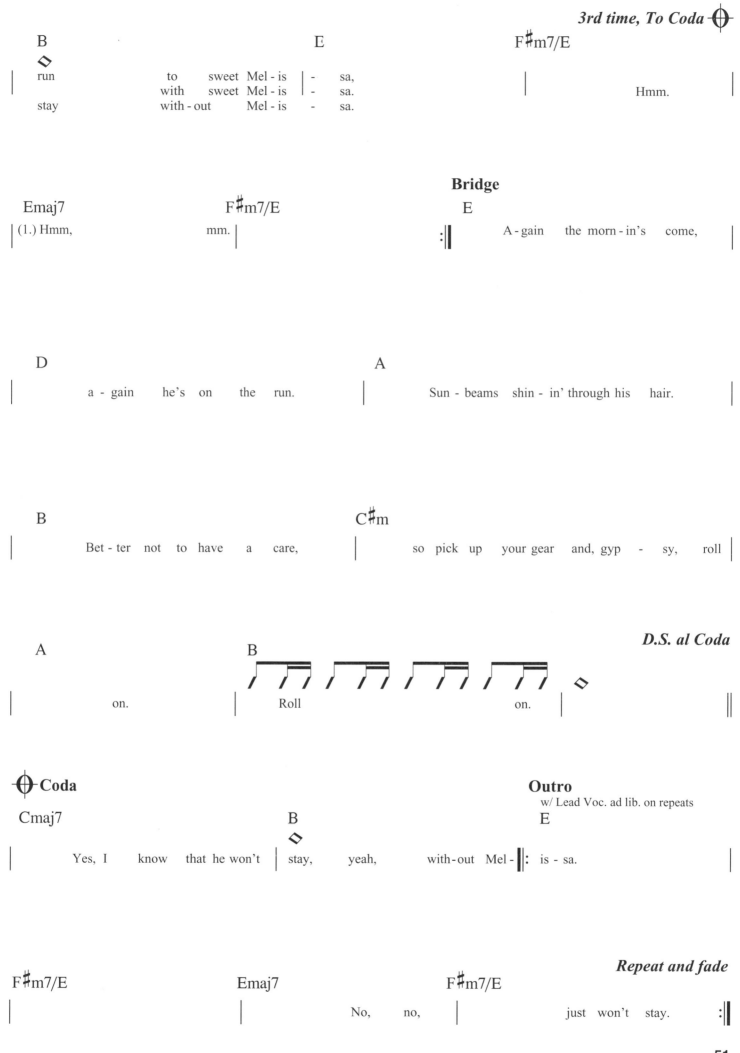

More Than a Feeling

Words and Music by Tom Scholz

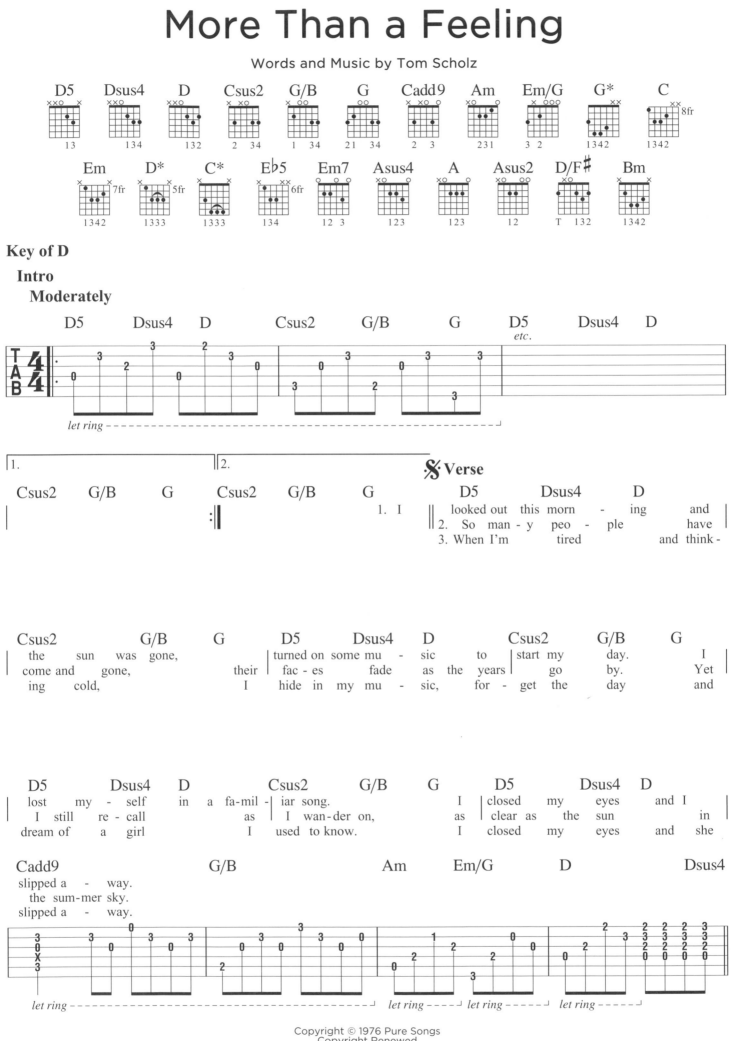

Key of D

Intro

Moderately

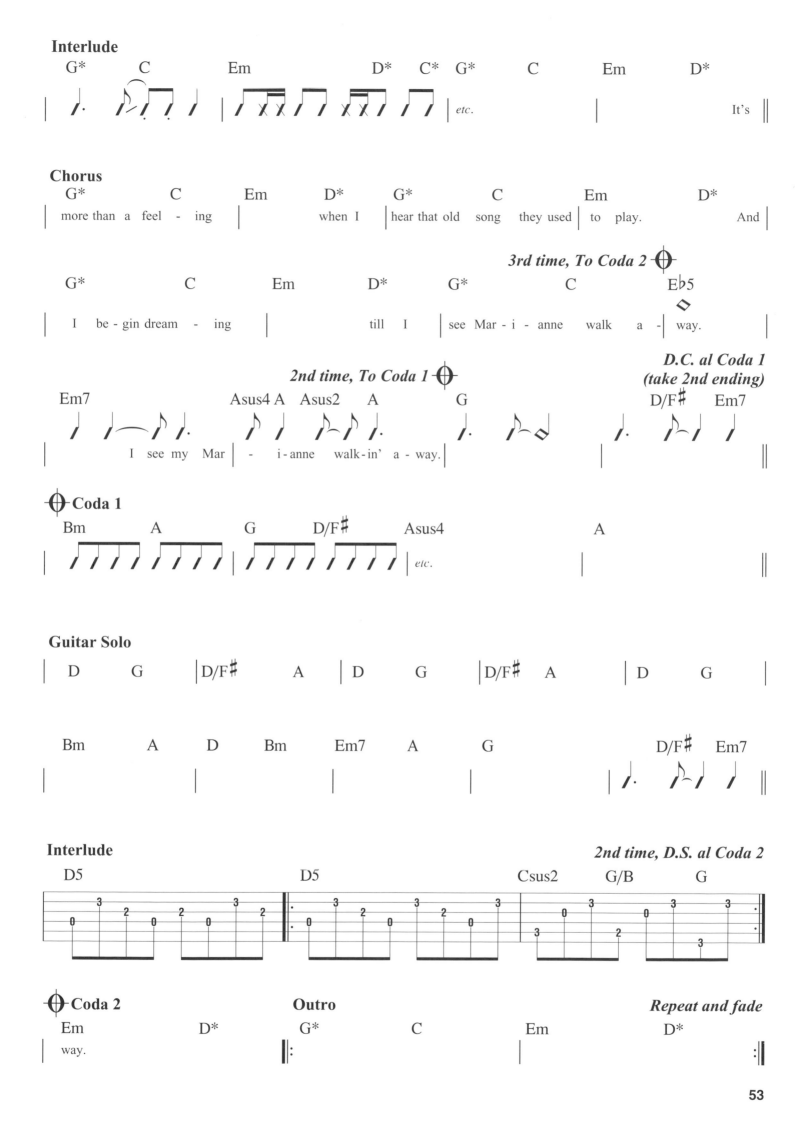

Interlude

G* C Em D* C* G* C Em D*

etc. It's

Chorus

G* C Em D* G* C Em D*

| more than a feel - ing | when I | hear that old song they used | to play. And |

3rd time, To Coda 2

G* C Em D* G* C Eb5

| I be - gin dream - ing | till I | see Mar - i - anne walk a - way. |

2nd time, To Coda 1   *D.C. al Coda 1 (take 2nd ending)*

Em7 Asus4 A Asus2 A G D/F# Em7

| I see my Mar | - i - anne walk - in' a - way. | |

Coda 1

Bm A G D/F# Asus4 A

etc.

Guitar Solo

| D G | D/F# A | D G | D/F# A | D G |

Bm A D Bm Em7 A G D/F# Em7

Interlude

2nd time, D.S. al Coda 2

D5 D5 Csus2 G/B G

Coda 2 **Outro** *Repeat and fade*

Em D* G* C Em D*

| way. |

More Than Words

Words and Music by Nuno Bettencourt and Gary Cherone

Chords: G G/B Cadd9 Am7 C D Dsus4 Em Em/B D7

D/F# G7 G7/B Cm Em7 Bm D7b9/A Dsus2/F Esus4 Gm/Bb

Tune down 1/2 step:
(low to high) Eb-Ab-Db-Gb-Bb-Eb

Key of G

Intro

Moderately slow

G   G/B   Cadd9   Am7   C   D Dsus4 G

```
  *                                                                        **
3 3 X      3 X        3 X   3 3 X   1      0 X    3  1 1 1      0 X  2      3 X 3
3 3 X 3    3 X X      3 0 X 3 3 X          1 X    0  1          1 X  3      3 X 3
0   X 0    0 X X      2   X             0  0 X    0  2  2 2  2  2 X     2   0
                        2   X          0  2 X      3            X
  3          2             3 3 3   X   0          0 0 0   X   3               3
```
w/ fingers

*Hit muted strings w/ R.H. throughout.

**Hold into beat 1
on repeat.

𝄋 Verse
etc.

G   G/B   Cadd9   Am7   C   D   Dsus4 G
1. Say - in', "I   love   you," is   not the words I   want   to   hear from you.
2. Now that I've   tried   to   talk to   you and   make you   un - der - stand,

G/B   Cadd9   Am7   C   D   Dsus4 Em
It's not that I   want   you   not to   say,   but   if   you   on - ly   knew
all   you   have   to do is close   your eyes and just reach out   your   hands

Em/B   Am7   D7   G   D/F#   Em
how   eas - y   it   would be   to   show   me   how   you   feel.
and   touch me.   Hold me close, don't ev   l- er   let   me   go.

Chorus

Em/B   Am7   D7   G7
More than   words   is   all   you   have   to   do
More than   words   is   all   I   ev - er need -

G7/B   C   Cm   G
to   make   it   real.   Then you   would -n't have   to   say
-ed   you   to   show.

Em7   Am7   D7   ***(D7b9/A)
that you   love   me   'cause I'd   al - read - y
                                                    ***2nd time only

G   G/B   G   G/B   D/F#   Em   Bm   C
know. What would you   do   if my heart was torn in   two?

Copyright © 1990 COLOR ME BLIND MUSIC
All Rights Administered by ALMO MUSIC CORP.
All Rights Reserved Used by Permission

54

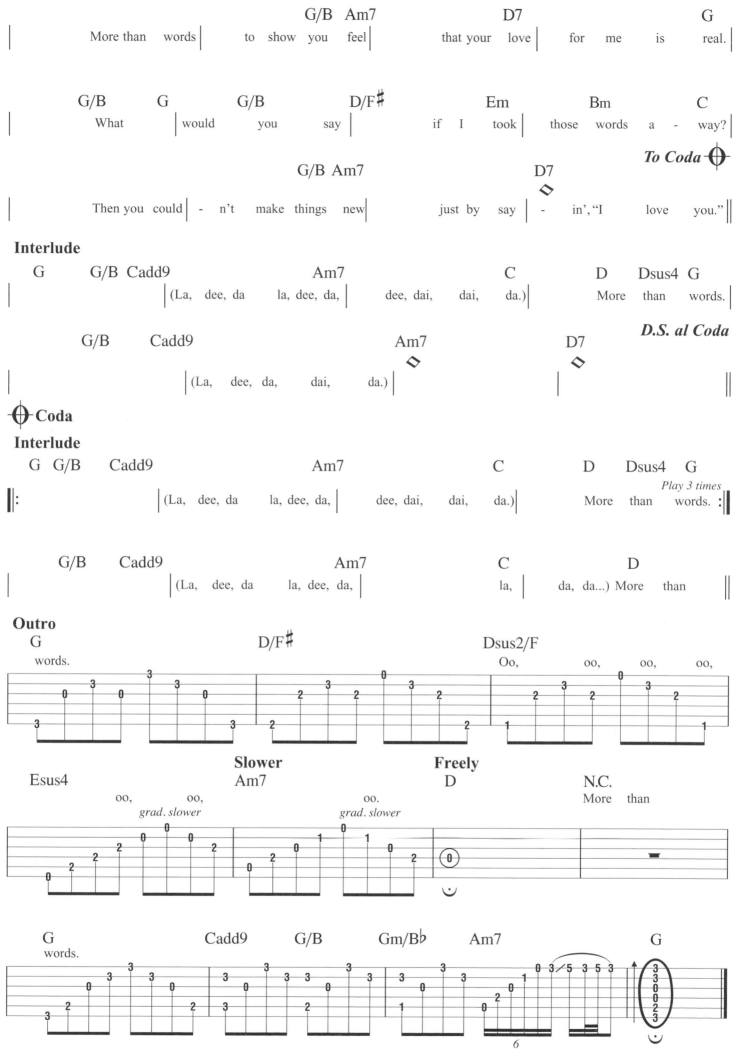

G/B Am7   D7   G
More than words| to show you feel| that your love| for me is real.|

G/B   G   G/B   D/F♯   Em   Bm   C
What |would   you   say | if I took| those words a - way?|

To Coda

G/B Am7   D7
Then you could|-n't make things new   just by say|-in', "I love you."‖

Interlude

G   G/B Cadd9   Am7   C   D   Dsus4 G
    |(La, dee, da   la, dee, da,| dee, dai, dai, da.)| More than words.|

D.S. al Coda

G/B   Cadd9   Am7   D7
| (La,   dee, da,   dai, da.)| | ‖

Coda

Interlude

G G/B Cadd9   Am7   C   D   Dsus4 G
                                                              Play 3 times
‖: |(La, dee, da   la, dee, da,| dee, dai, dai, da.)| More than words. :‖

G/B   Cadd9   Am7   C   D
| (La, dee, da   la, dee, da,| la,| da, da...) More than   ‖

Outro

G   D/F♯   Dsus2/F
words.   Oo,   oo,   oo,   oo,

Esus4   Am7   D   N.C.
oo,   oo,   oo.   More   than
grad. slower   *grad. slower*

G   Cadd9   G/B   Gm/B♭   Am7   G
words.

Nothing Else Matters

Words and Music by James Hetfield and Lars Ulrich

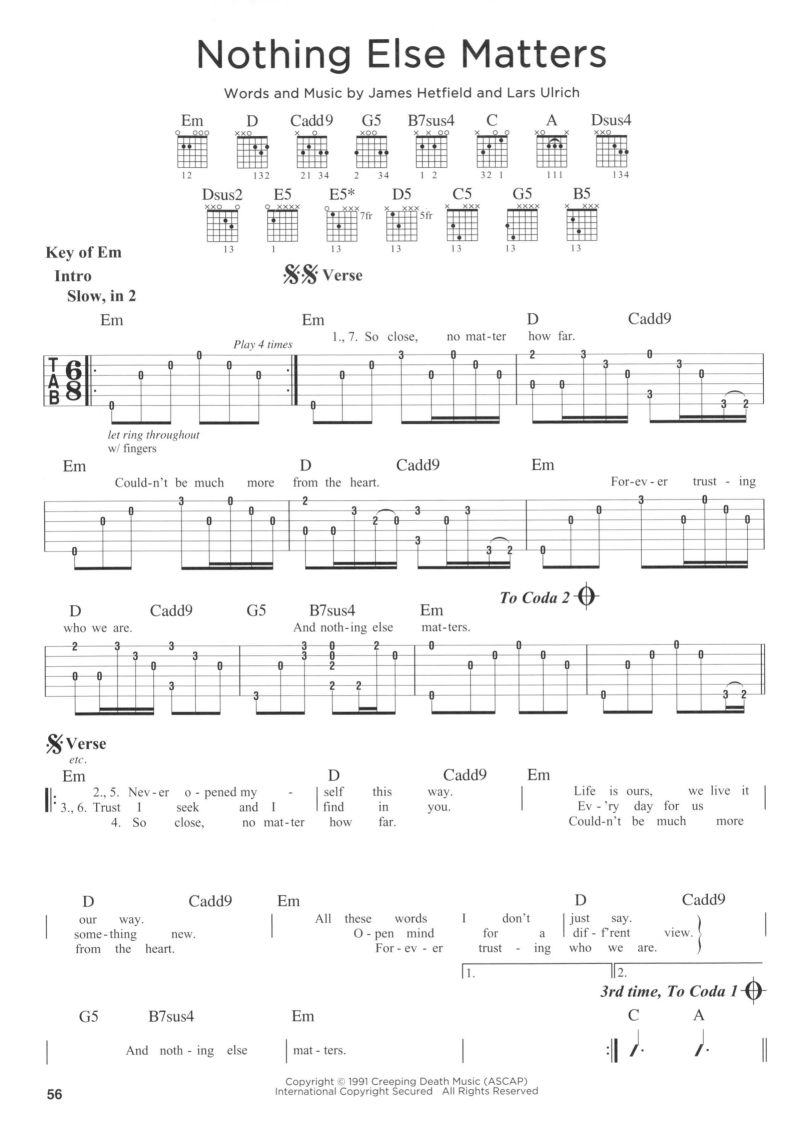

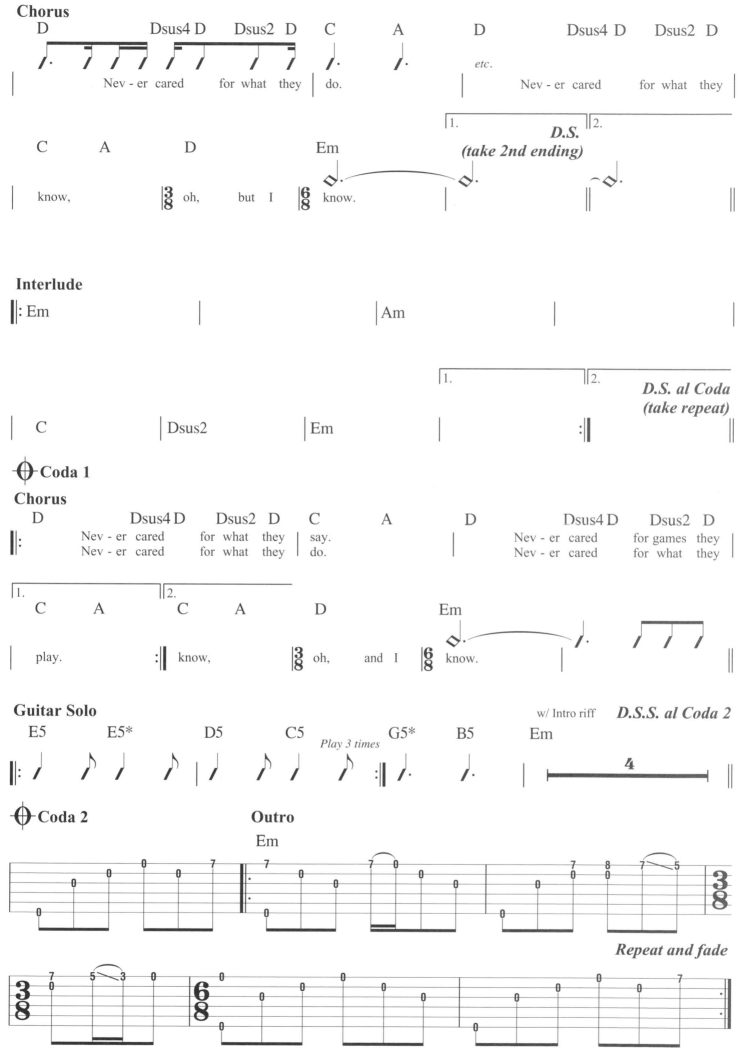

One

Lyrics by Bono and The Edge
Music by U2

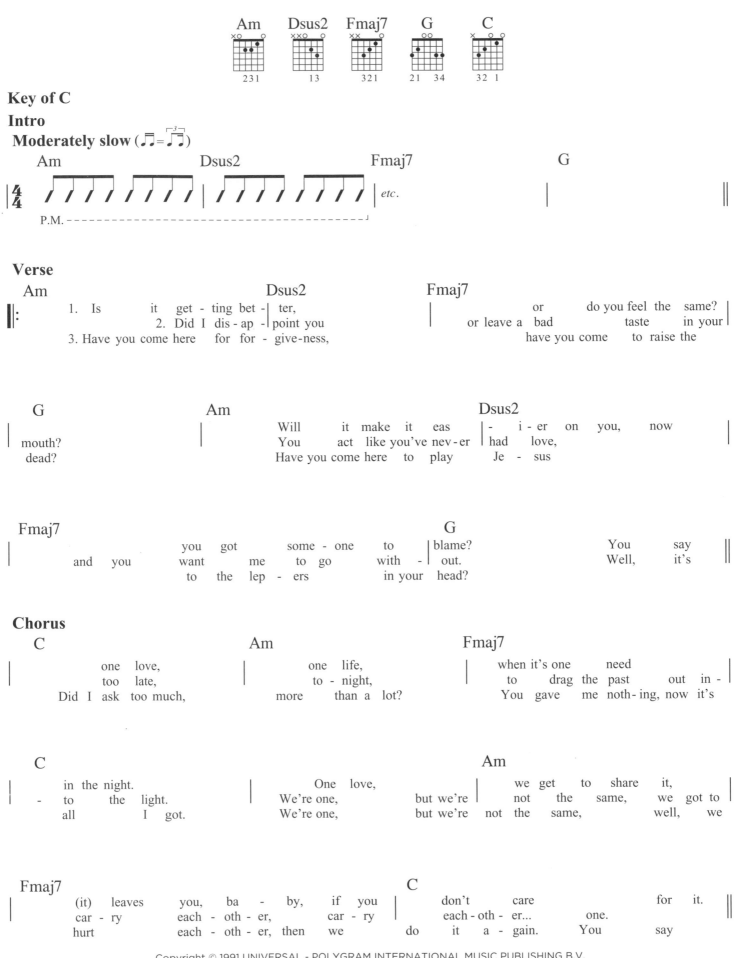

1., 2.

Interlude

| Am | Dsus2 | Fmaj7 | G |

etc.

3.

Bridge

| C | | Am | | C | |
| love is a tem - ple, love | a high - er law, | love | is a tem - ple, love |

| Am | | C | | G | |
| the high - er law. You ask | me to en - ter, but | then you make me crawl, and |

| | | Fmaj7 | | | |
| I can't be hold - ing on | to what you've got | when all you've got is hurt. |

Chorus

| C | | Am | | Fmaj7 | |
| One love, | one blood, | one life, you got to |

| C | | | | Am | |
| do what you should. | One life, | with each - oth - er: |

| Fmaj7 | | C | | | |
| sis - ters, | broth - ers. | One life but we're |

| Am | | Fmaj7 | | C | |
| not the same, we get to | car - ry each - oth - er, car - ry | each - oth - er. One, |

Outro

w/ Lead Voc. ad lib. on repeats

| C | Am | Fmaj7 | C | *Play 4 times* |
| Ah, ah. | one. | | |

| | Am | Fmaj7 | C |
| Ah, ah. | Oh, ah, | ah. | Yeah. |

Patience

Words and Music by W. Axl Rose, Slash, Izzy Stradlin', Duff McKagan and Steven Adler

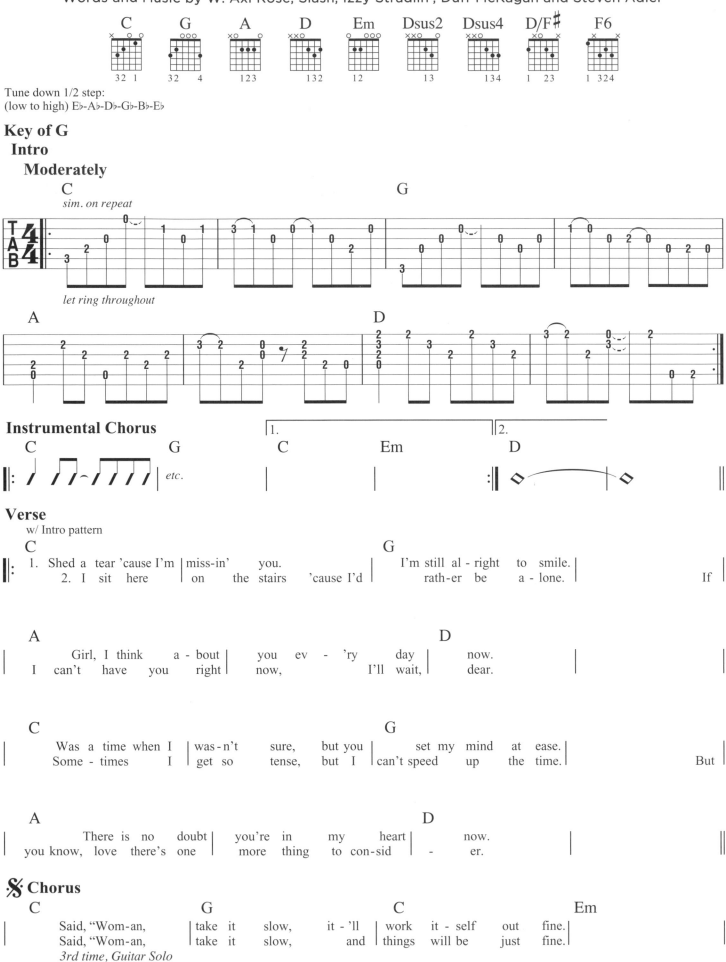

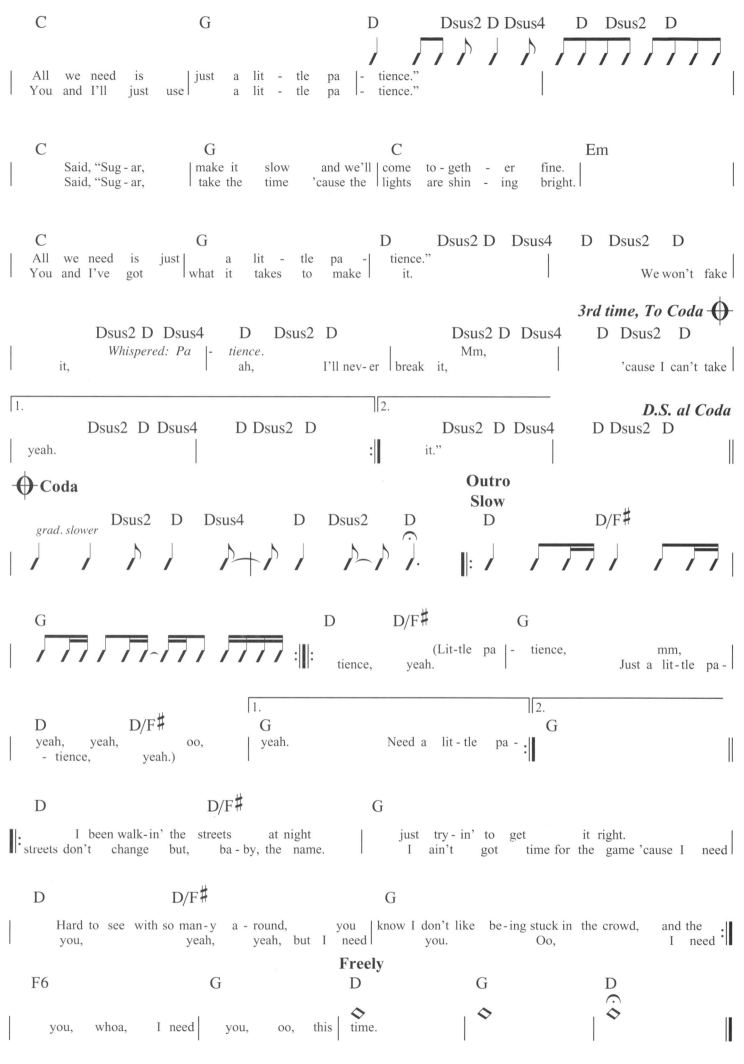

C   G   D   Dsus2 D Dsus4 D Dsus2 D

All we need is |just a lit - tle pa |- tience."
You and I'll just use| a lit - tle pa |- tience."

C   G   C   Em

Said, "Sug - ar, |make it slow and we'll |come to - geth - er fine.
Said, "Sug - ar, |take the time 'cause the |lights are shin - ing bright.|

C   G   D   Dsus2 D Dsus4 D Dsus2 D

All we need is just| a lit - tle pa - |tience."
You and I've got |what it takes to make | it.   We won't fake

3rd time, To Coda ⊕

Dsus2 D Dsus4 D Dsus2 D   Dsus2 D Dsus4 D Dsus2 D

 Whispered: Pa |- *tience.*   Mm,
it,   ah, I'll nev - er |break it,   'cause I can't take

1.   2.   ***D.S. al Coda***

Dsus2 D Dsus4 D Dsus2 D   Dsus2 D Dsus4 D Dsus2 D

yeah.   it."

⊕ **Coda**

                            Outro
                            Slow

grad. slower Dsus2 D Dsus4 D Dsus2 D   D   D/F♯

G   D D/F♯   G

                      tience,   yeah.   (Lit - tle pa |- tience,   mm,   Just a lit - tle pa -

1.   2.

D   D/F♯   G   G

yeah, yeah,   oo, | yeah.   Need a lit - tle pa -
- tience, yeah.)

D   D/F♯   G

   I been walk-in' the streets at night | just try - in' to get   it right.
streets don't change but, ba - by, the name. | I ain't got time for the game 'cause I need

D   D/F♯   G

Hard to see with so man-y a - round, you |know I don't like be - ing stuck in the crowd, and the
you,   yeah,   yeah, but I need| you.   Oo,   I need

                        Freely

F6   G   D   G   D

 you, whoa, I need| you, oo, this | time.

61

Peaceful Easy Feeling

Words and Music by Jack Tempchin

E   Esus4   A   B7   F#m11

231   234   234   213 4   2 34

Key of E
Intro
Moderately fast

E   Esus4   *Play 4 times*

| 4/4 | / / / / / / / | / / / / ~ ♪ / / ♪ | :||

𝄋 Verse

*E   A   E   A
etc.

||: 1. I   like   the   way | your spark - ling ear | - rings | lay |
2. And I found | out   a   long | time | a - go |
3. I get this | feel - in' I may know | you |

*3rd time, let chords ring, next 2 meas.

E   A   B7

a - gainst your	skin so brown.	
what a wom-an can do	to your soul,	
as a lov - er and a friend,	

E   A   E   A

And I wan - na	sleep with you in the	des - ert to - night	
ah, but she	can't take you	an - y - way	
but this voice keeps	whis - per - ing in my oth - er ear,	tells me

E   A   B7

| with a bil - lion | stars all a - round. | 'Cause I got a }||
| you don't al-read-y know | how to go. | And I got a }
| I may nev - er | see you a - gain. | 'Cause I get a }

Chorus

A   E

| peace - ful | eas - y feel | - ing, | |

A   F#m11   B7

| and I know you won't | let me down, | 'cause I'm |

3rd time, To Coda ⊕

E   F#m11   A   B7

| al - | read - y stand - ing | on the ground. |

| E | Esus4 | E | Esus4 :‖

Guitar Solo

‖: E | A | E | A |

| E | A | B7 | :‖

| A | | E | |

| A | | B7 | |

D.S. al Coda

| E | F#m11 | A | B7 ‖

⊕ **Coda**

B7   E   F#m11   A   B7
| I'm | al   - | read-y | stand - ing. | Yes, I'm |

E   F#m11   A   B7
| al   - | read-y | stand - ing | on   the   ground. ‖

Outro

E   F#m11   A   B7   E
                                                        Play 3 times
‖: | | | :‖ ◊ ‖

63

Redemption Song

Words and Music by Bob Marley

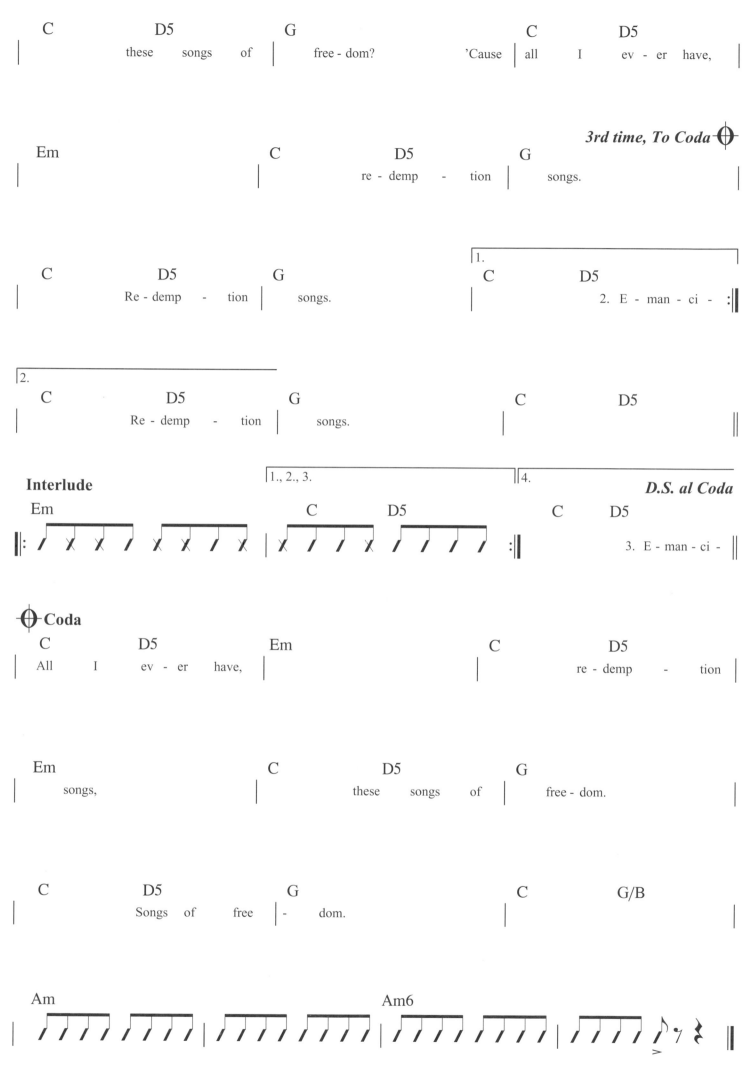

Ring of Fire

Words and Music by Merle Kilgore and June Carter

Key of G
Intro
 Very fast
 Half-time feel

G   C   D7

Verse

|G | | C G | $\frac{2}{4}$ | $\frac{4}{4}$ | | |
| 1. Love | | is a burn-ing | thing | | | | and it |

| | | D7 G | $\frac{2}{4}$ | $\frac{4}{4}$ | | |
| makes | | a fier - y | ring. | | | | |

| | | C G | $\frac{2}{4}$ | $\frac{4}{4}$ | | |
| Bound | | by wild de - | sires, | | | | |

| | | D7 | $\frac{2}{4}$ | G | $\frac{4}{4}$ | |
| I fell in - to a | | ring of | fire. | | | |

𝄋 Chorus

D7   C   G
| I fell | in - to a | burn-ing ring of | fire. I went |

D7   C   G
| down, down, | down, and the | flames went | high - er. And it |

                                            D7 G
| burns, burns, | burns, | the ring of | fire, |

To Coda ⊕

D7   G
| the ring of | fire. |

Copyright © 1962, 1963 Painted Desert Music Corporation, New York
Copyright Renewed
International Copyright Secured   All Rights Reserved
Used by Permission

66

Interlude

‖: G |2/4 C |4/4 G |

2nd time, D.S. al Coda

| |2/4 D7 |4/4 G | :‖

⊕ **Coda**   **Verse**

     G   C   G   C   G
| 2. The ‖taste | of love is |sweet |2/4 |4/4 |

     D7   G   D7   G
| when |hearts | like ours |meet. |2/4 |4/4 |

     C   G   C   G
| | I fell for you |2/4 like a |4/4 child. | |2/4 |4/4 |

     D7   G
| |Oh, | but the fire went |wild. | ‖

Outro-Chorus

D7   C   G
‖: I fell | in - to a |burn-ing ring of | fire. I went |

D7   C   G
| down, down, |down, and the |flames went |high - er. And it |

     D7   G
| burns, burns, |burns, | the ring of | fire, |

          1.   2.
D7   G
| the ring of | fire. | :‖ And it |

     D7   G   D7
| burns, burns, |burns, | the ring of | fire, | the ring of ‖

Repeat and fade

G   D7   G   D7
‖: fire, | the ring of | fire, | the ring of :‖

Run Around

Words and Music by John Popper

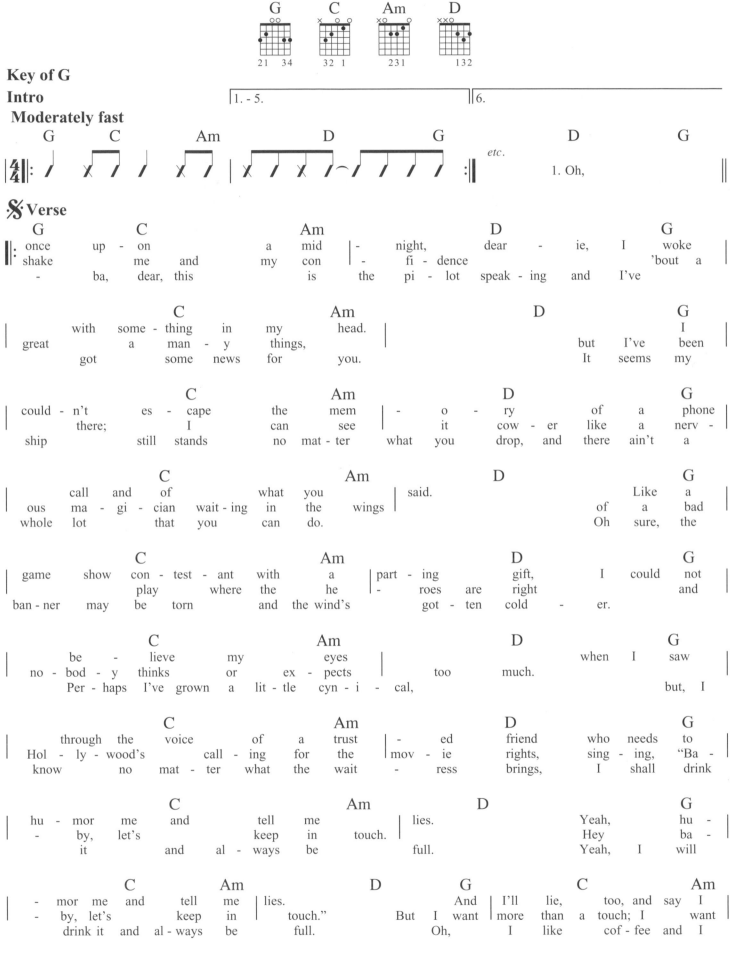

| D   G   C   Am   D   G
don't mind. And	as we seek, so	shall we find. And
you to reach me and	show me all the things no one else	we can see, so
like tea. But to	be a - ble to en - ter a fi -	nal plea. I

| C   Am   D   G
when you're feel - ing o - pen I'll still be	here, but
what you feel be - comes mine	as a well. And
still got this dream that you just can't	shake. I

| C   Am   D   G
not with - out a cer - tain de - gree	of fear of
soon, if we're luck - y, we'd be un -	a - ble to tell what's
love you to the point you can no long - er	take. Well, all right,

| C   Am   D   G
| what will   be   with | you   and   me.   I   still |
| yours and   mine,   the | fish - ing's fine,   and   it   does - |
| o - kay,   so   be that   way.   I |

| C   Am   D   G
| n't can   see   things,   hope | - ful - ly. ||
| n't have to rhyme, so don't you | feed me   a   line. } But   you, ||
| hope and   pray that there's some - thing left to say.) |

Chorus
| G   C Am   D   G   C   Am   D   G
| | why you wan-na | give me a run a - round? | Is   it a sure |

To Coda ⊕

| C   Am   D   G   C   Am   D   G
| - fire way to speed| things up,   when| all it does is   slow | me |

| 1. | 2.
| C   Am   D   G   D   G
| down? | 2. But :|| D   G ||

Harmonica Solo   *D.S. al Coda*
| 1. - 5. | 6.
| G   C Am   D   G   D   G
||: | :|| 3. Tra - la - la bom - ||

⊕**Coda**
| C   Am   D   G   C   Am   D   G
| all it does is   slow me |down?   Oh, | you. | Why   you wan - na |

| C   Am   D   G   C   Am   D   G
| give me a run a - round? | Is   it a sure | - fire way to speed| things up   when |

| C   Am   D   G   C   Am   D   G
| all it does is   slow | me |down? | ||

Outro-Harmonica Solo   *Repeat and fade*
||: G   C   Am| D   G | C   Am| D   G :||

69

Signs

Words and Music by Les Emmerson

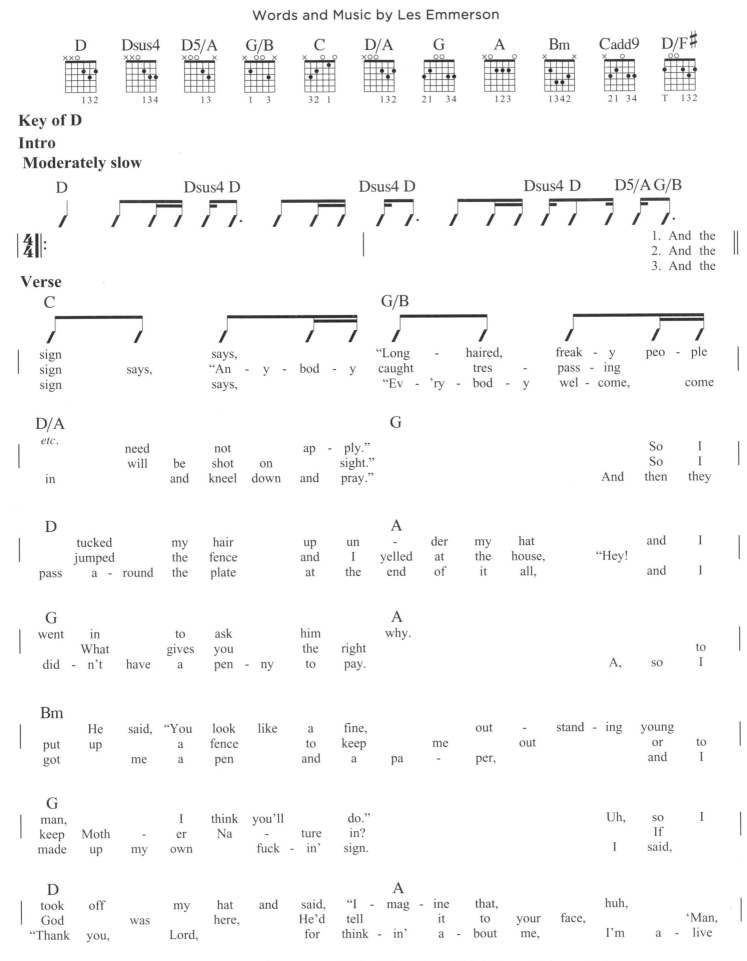

Key of D

Intro

Moderately slow

Verse

1. And the sign says, "Long-haired, freak-y peo-ple need not ap-ply." So I tucked my hair up un-der my hat and I went in to ask him why. He said, "You look like a fine, out-stand-ing young man, I think you'll do." Uh, so I took off my hat and said, "I-mag-ine that, huh,

2. And the sign says, "An-y-bod-y caught tres-pass-ing will be shot on sight." So I jumped the fence and I yelled at the house, "Hey! What gives you the right to put up a fence to keep me out or to keep Moth-er Na-ture in? If God was here, He'd tell it to your face, 'Man,

3. And the sign says, "Ev-'ry-bod-y wel-come, come in and kneel down and pray." And then they pass a-round the plate at the end of it all, and I did-n't have a pen-ny to pay. So I got me a pen and a pa-per, and I made up my own fuck-in' sign. I said, "Thank you, Lord, for think-in' a-bout me, I'm a-live

G   A
me   a   work - ing   for   you."   Oh.
     you're some   kind   of   sin - ner.'"   Oh.
     and   do - in'   fine."   Oh.

Chorus

D   Cadd9   G   D   G
Signs,   signs,   ev - 'ry-where a sign fuck | - ing up the scen-er - y, break - ing my mind.

3rd time, To Coda ⊕ ⌐1.

D   A   Cadd9
Do this, don't   do   that.   Can't you read   the sign?

⌐2.

Cadd9   D   Dsus4 D/F♯ G   G♯   A
                                                                      ⑥
                                                                      4fr

                                                        Oh.   Uh,

Bridge

A   G   D   Dsus4 D
say now,   mis - ter, can't   you read?   You | got to have a shirt and tie   to get a seat.

                                                        w/ Intro pattern
             A   G   D   Dsus4 D
You can't watch,   no   you   can't eat.   **2/4** You ain't sup-posed to **4/4** be   here.

Dsus4 D   Dsus4 D   N.C.
                                          And the | sign   said, "You got to have a mem - ber - ship

Guitar Solo
                                          D   Cadd9   G
card   to get in - side."   Oo! ‖

                                                        D.C. al Coda
D   G | D   A | Cadd9   ‖

⊕ **Coda**

Cadd9   D   Cadd9   G
                                  | Signs,   signs,   ev - 'ry-where a sign fuck -

D   G   D   A
- ing up the scen-er - y, break - ing my mind. | Do this, don't   do that.   Can't you read   the sign?

Cadd9   D
                                             ◊

71

Silent Lucidity

Words and Music by Chris DeGarmo

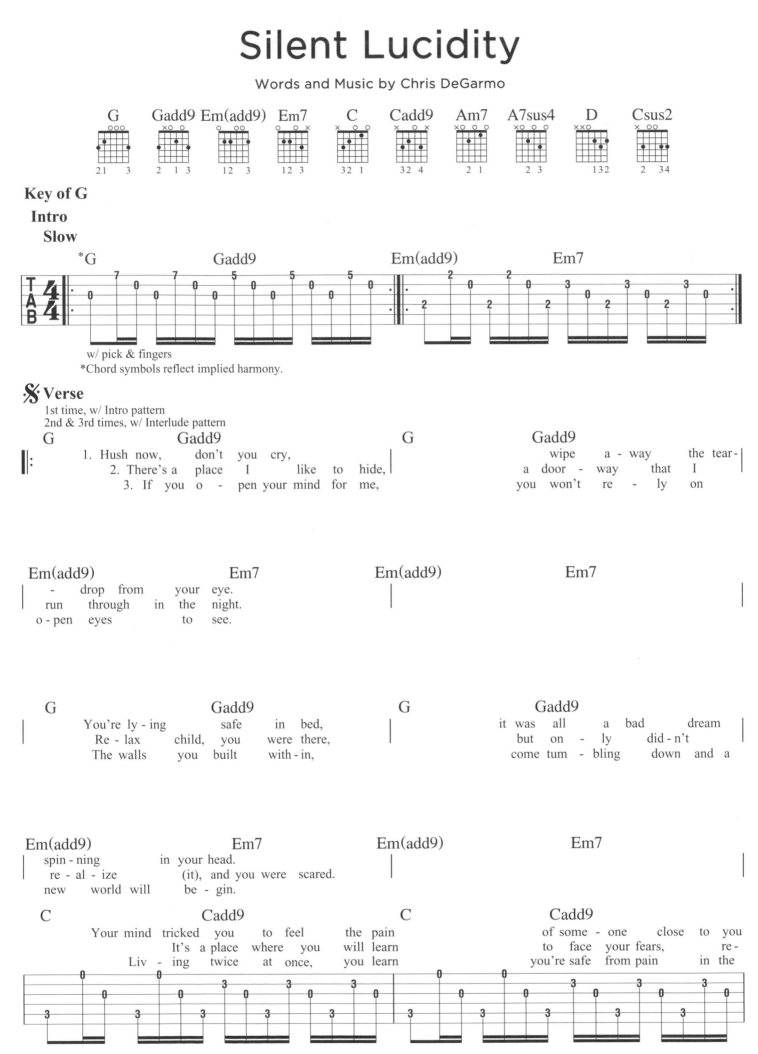

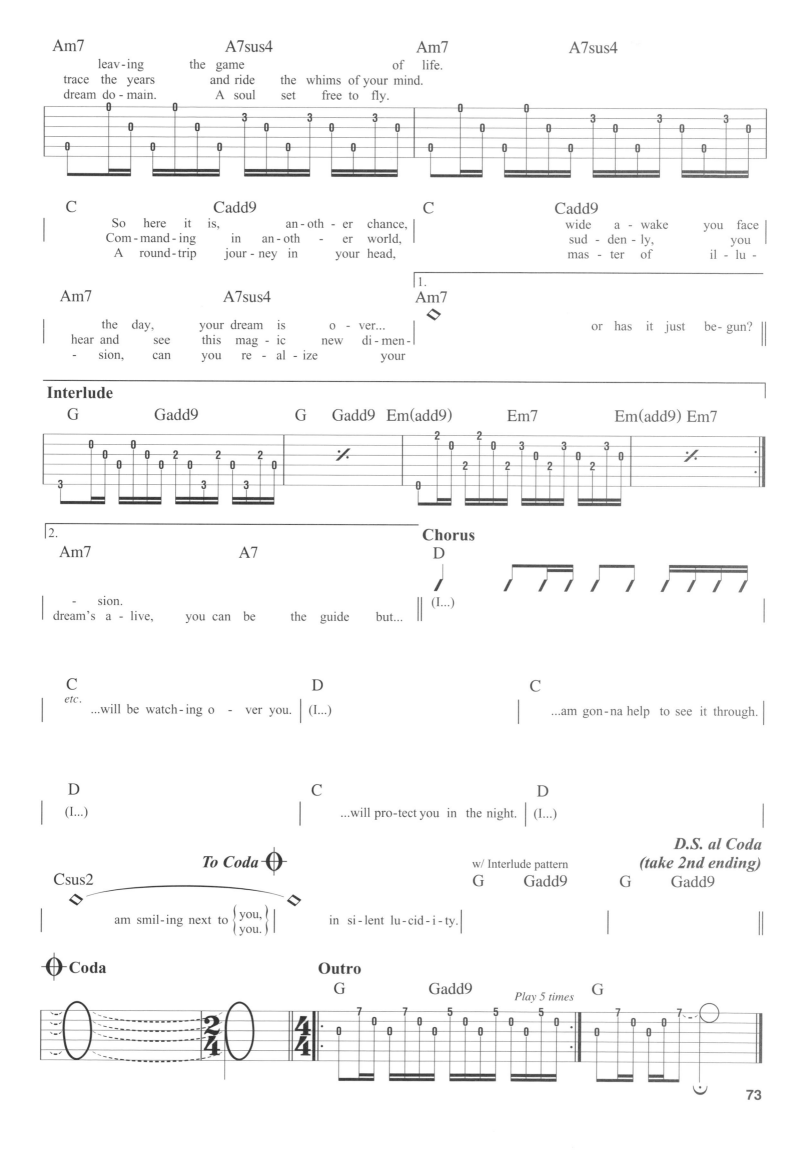

Stairway to Heaven

Words and Music by Jimmy Page and Robert Plant

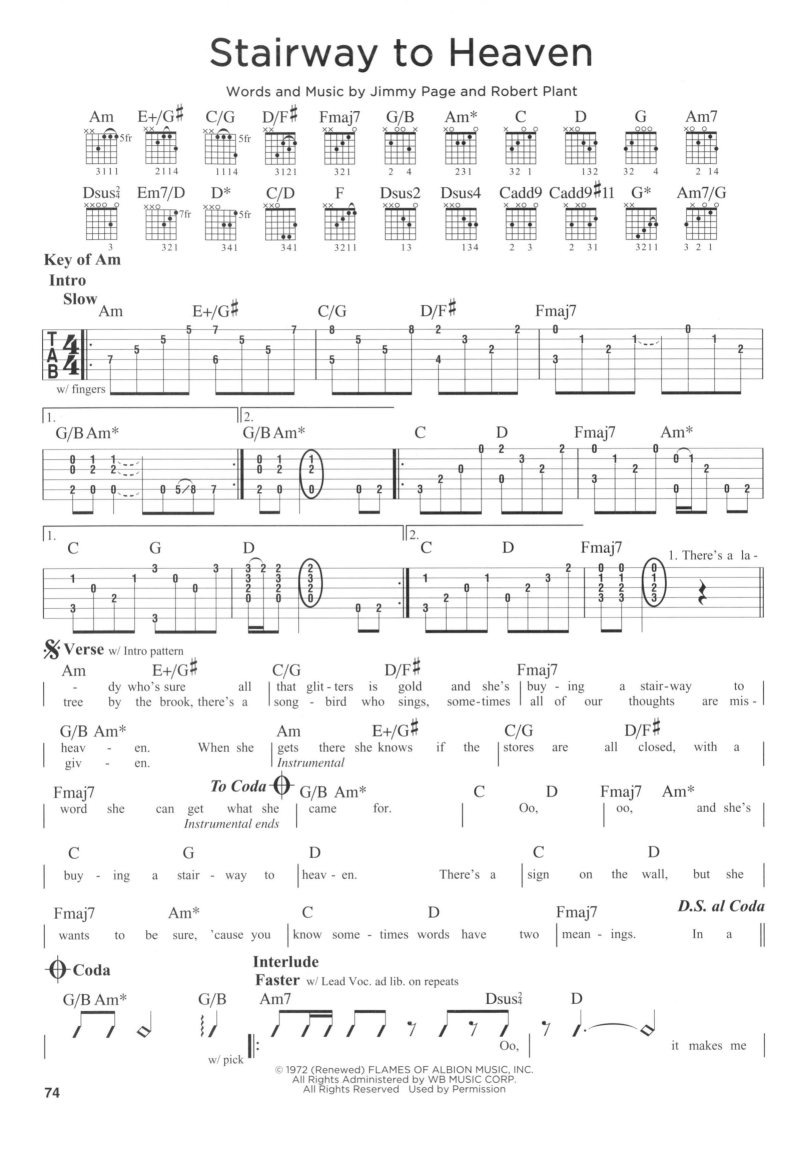

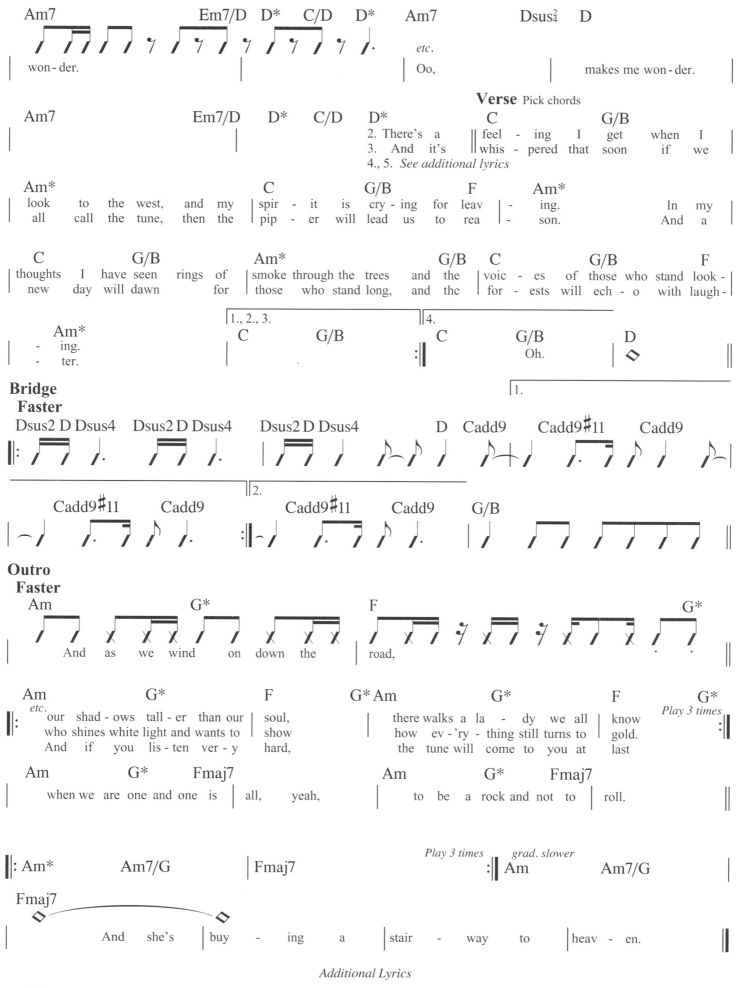

Additional Lyrics

4. If there's a bustle in your hedge-row, don't be alarmed now,
It's just a spring clean for the May queen.
Yes, there are two paths you can go by, but in the long run,
There's still time to change the road you're on.

5. Your head is humming and it won't go, in case you don't know,
The piper's calling you to join him.
Dear lady, can you hear the wind blow, and did you know,
Your stairway lies on the whisp'ring wind.

Take Me Home, Country Roads

Words and Music by John Denver, Bill Danoff and Taffy Nivert

Key of A

Intro

Moderately slow, in 2

Verse

let ring throughout

etc.

Chorus

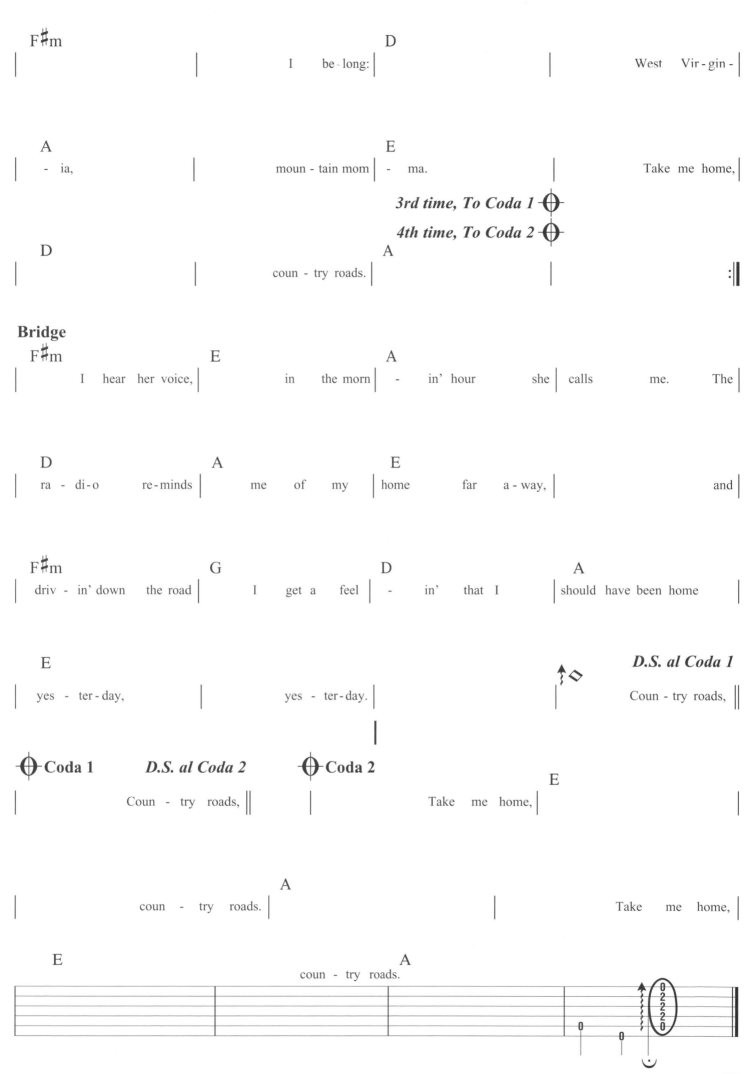

77

Tangled Up in Blue

Words and Music by Bob Dylan

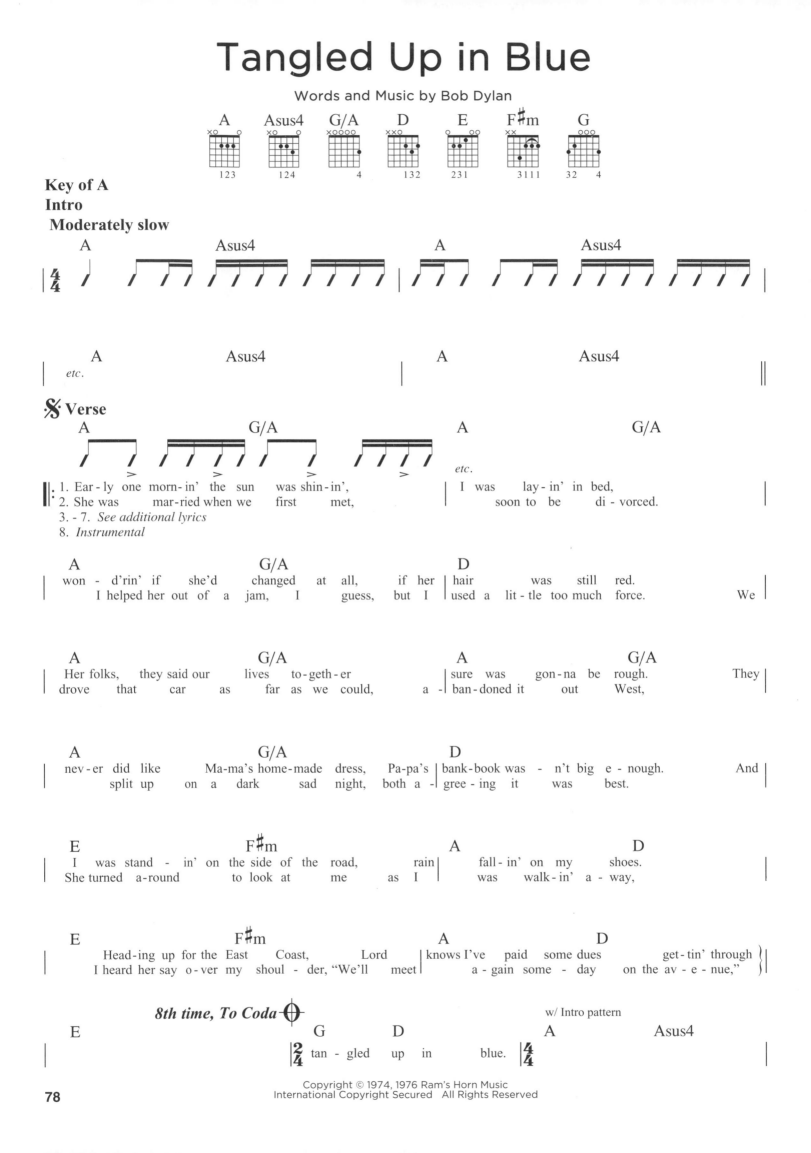

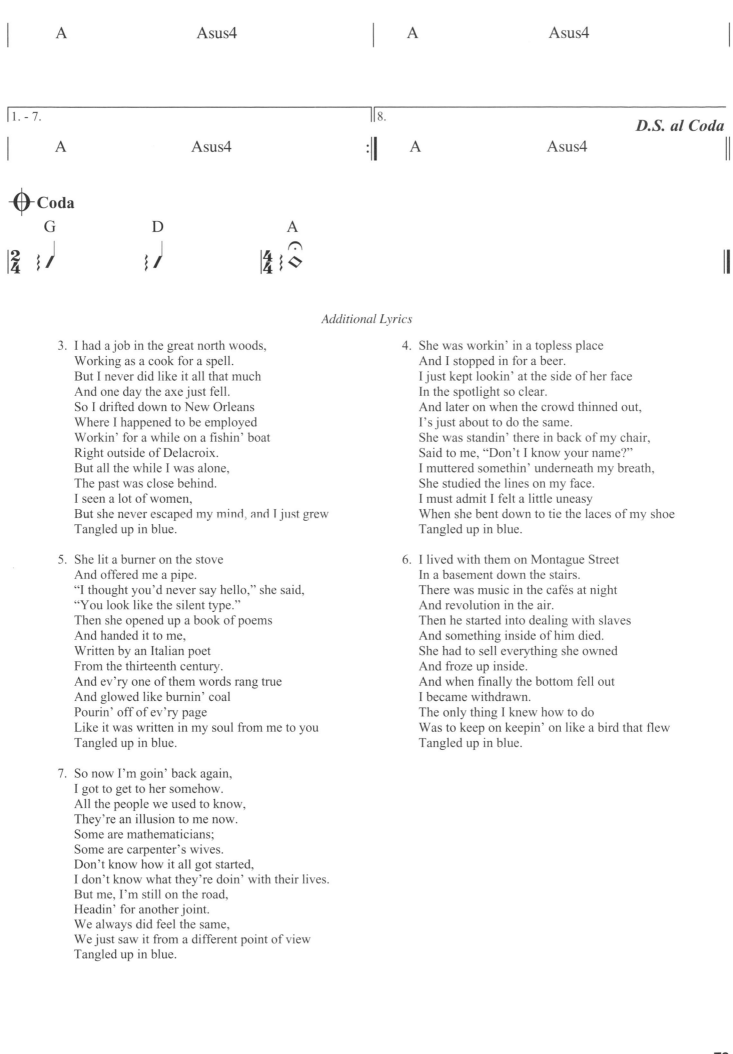

D.S. al Coda

Coda

Additional Lyrics

3. I had a job in the great north woods,
   Working as a cook for a spell.
   But I never did like it all that much
   And one day the axe just fell.
   So I drifted down to New Orleans
   Where I happened to be employed
   Workin' for a while on a fishin' boat
   Right outside of Delacroix.
   But all the while I was alone,
   The past was close behind.
   I seen a lot of women,
   But she never escaped my mind, and I just grew
   Tangled up in blue.

5. She lit a burner on the stove
   And offered me a pipe.
   "I thought you'd never say hello," she said,
   "You look like the silent type."
   Then she opened up a book of poems
   And handed it to me,
   Written by an Italian poet
   From the thirteenth century.
   And ev'ry one of them words rang true
   And glowed like burnin' coal
   Pourin' off of ev'ry page
   Like it was written in my soul from me to you
   Tangled up in blue.

7. So now I'm goin' back again,
   I got to get to her somehow.
   All the people we used to know,
   They're an illusion to me now.
   Some are mathematicians;
   Some are carpenter's wives.
   Don't know how it all got started,
   I don't know what they're doin' with their lives.
   But me, I'm still on the road,
   Headin' for another joint.
   We always did feel the same,
   We just saw it from a different point of view
   Tangled up in blue.

4. She was workin' in a topless place
   And I stopped in for a beer.
   I just kept lookin' at the side of her face
   In the spotlight so clear.
   And later on when the crowd thinned out,
   I's just about to do the same.
   She was standin' there in back of my chair,
   Said to me, "Don't I know your name?"
   I muttered somethin' underneath my breath,
   She studied the lines on my face.
   I must admit I felt a little uneasy
   When she bent down to tie the laces of my shoe
   Tangled up in blue.

6. I lived with them on Montague Street
   In a basement down the stairs.
   There was music in the cafés at night
   And revolution in the air.
   Then he started into dealing with slaves
   And something inside of him died.
   She had to sell everything she owned
   And froze up inside.
   And when finally the bottom fell out
   I became withdrawn.
   The only thing I knew how to do
   Was to keep on keepin' on like a bird that flew
   Tangled up in blue.

Tequila Sunrise

Words and Music by Don Henley and Glenn Frey

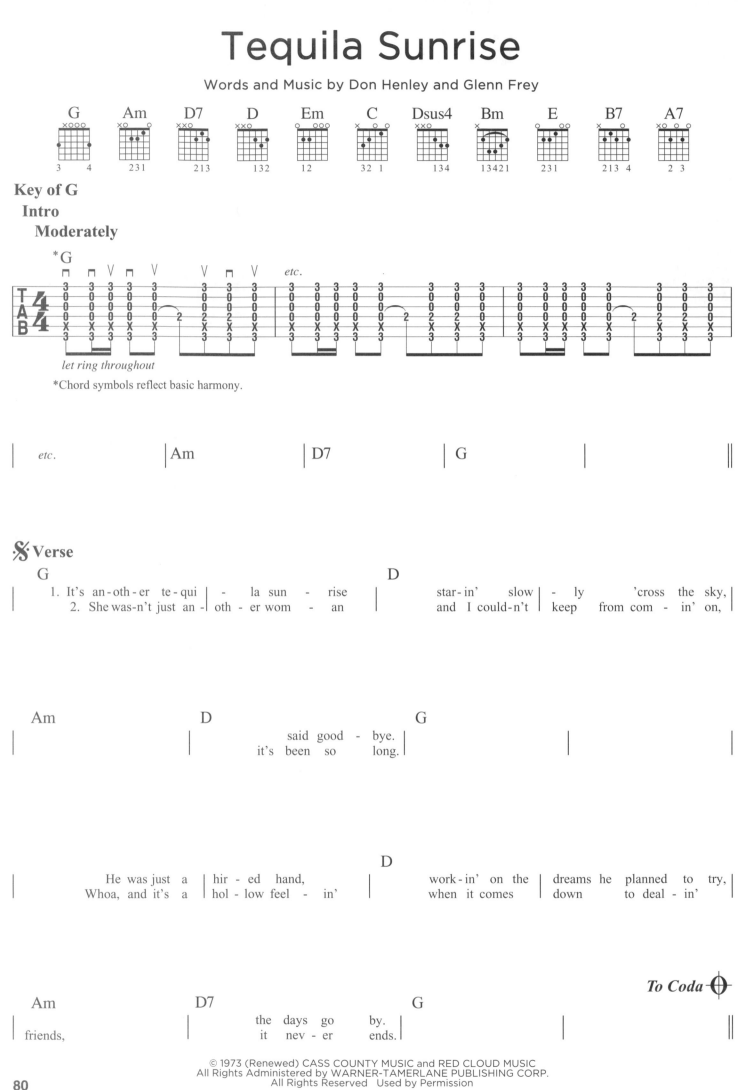

Chorus

Em		C		Em		C	

Ev-'ry night when the sun goes down, just an-oth-er lone-ly boy in town

D.S. al Coda

Em		Am		D	Dsus4	

and she's out run-nin' 'round.

⊕ Coda

Guitar Solo

G			D		

Am		D		G		

Bridge

Am	D		Bm	E	

Take an-oth-er shot of cour-age. Won-der why the right words nev-er come,

Am	B7		Em	A7	

you just get numb.

Verse

G		D		

3. And it's an-oth-er te-qui - la sun-rise, this old world still looks the same,

Am	D	G		

an-oth-er frame.

Outro

G			Mm.			

81

Trouble

Words and Music by Ray LaMontagne

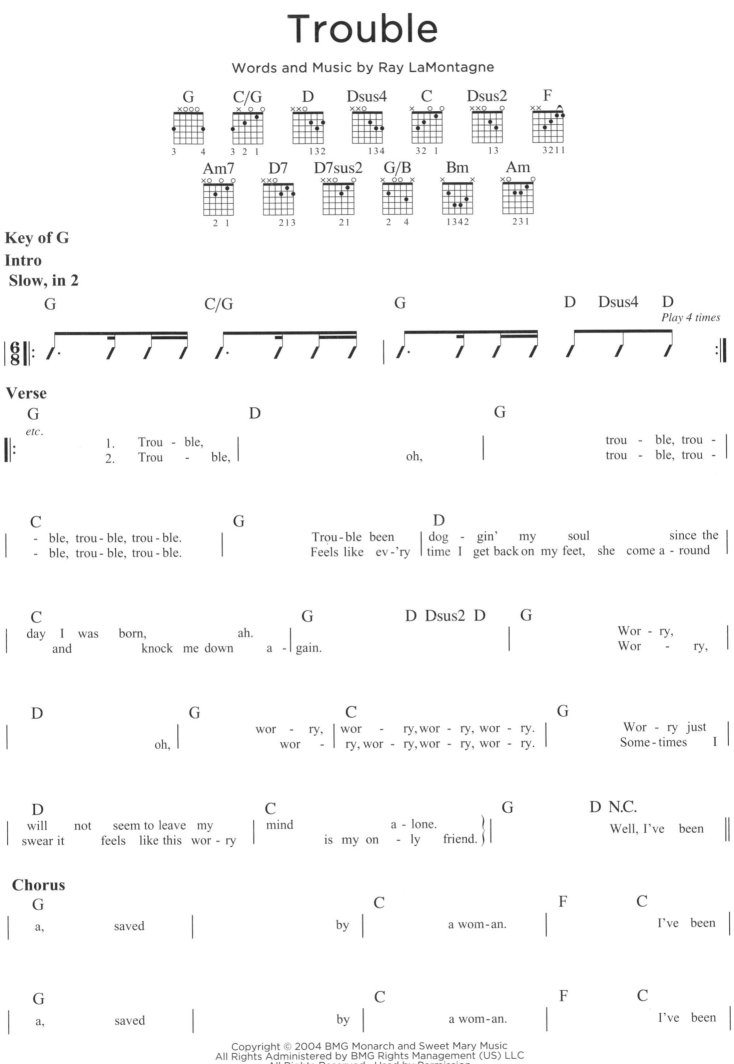

Key of G
Intro
  Slow, in 2

Play 4 times

Verse

1. Trou - ble,
2. Trou - ble,   oh,   trou - ble, trou -
                                          trou - ble, trou -

- ble, trou - ble, trou - ble.   Trou - ble been | dog - gin' my   soul   since the
- ble, trou - ble, trou - ble.   Feels like ev - 'ry | time I get back on my feet, she come a - round

day I was   born,   ah. | Wor - ry,
   and   knock me down a - | gain.   Wor - ry,

oh, | wor - ry, | wor - ry, wor - ry, wor - ry. | Wor - ry just
          wor - | ry, wor - ry, wor - ry, wor - ry. | Some - times I

will   not   seem to leave my | mind   a - lone.   G   D N.C.
swear it   feels like this wor - ry   is my on - ly   friend. } Well, I've been

Chorus

a,   saved | by | a wom - an. | I've been

a,   saved | by | a wom - an. | I've been

G			C	*F	**C
a, saved		by	a wom - an.		She won't

*2nd time, substitute C.

**2nd time, substitute G/B.

Am7		D7	D7sus4 D7 D7sus2	
let me go,		she won't	let me go, now.	She won't

Am7			D7	
let me go,		she won't	let me go now,	

1.   **2.**

Intro (2 times)

D7sus2

| now. | **4** :|| now. ||

Bridge

1.   **2.**

: C	Bm	Am	G	:|| Am
Oh.		Ah.			Mm, she

: G C/G	G C/G	G C/G
good	to me, now. She gave me	love and af-

1.   **2.**

G C/G	G C/G	G C/G
fec - tion. Say she :|| fec - tion. I said, I	love her. Yes, I

G C/G	G C/G	G C/G
love her. I said, I	love her. I said, I	love. She

G C/G	G C/G	G C/G
good	to me, now. She	good to me. She

Outro

G C/G	G C/G	G C/G	G C/G
good to me.	Mm,	mm,	mm,

G C/G	G C/G	G
mm.		*grad. slower*

Truckin'

Words and Music by Jerry Garcia, Robert Hunter, Phil Lesh and Bob Weir

E   A   B   G   D/F#   D   F#   B/F#

Key of E

Intro

Moderately

N.C.(E)

E

Riff

Play 4 times

End Riff

𝄋 Chorus

w/ riff

strum chords

E

A

1. Truck - in',   got my   chips cashed   in,   keep   truck - in',   like the
2. Dal - las   got a   soft ma - chine,   Hous - ton,   too close to
4., 5. *See additional lyrics*

B

doo - dah   man.   To - geth - er,   more or   less in   line.
New Or - leans.   New   York   got the   ways an'   means,   and

w/ riff

A

E

Just keep truck - in' on.
just won't let you be.

Verse

E

1. Ar - rows of ne - on and flash - ing mar quees out on   Main Street.   Chi -
2. Most of the cats that you meet on the street speak of   true   love.
4., 5. *See additional lyrics*

ca - go, New - York, De - troit and it's all on the   same street.   Your
Most of the time, they're sit - ting and cry - ing at   home.

typ - i - cal cit - y in - volved in a typ - i - cal   day - dream.
One of these days   they know they've got - ta get   go - in'

Hang it up and see what to - mor - row brings.
out of the door and down to the street all a - lone.

Bridge

strum chords

A

G   D/F#   A

Some - times the lights all   **2/4** shin - in' on   **4/4** me.

                                     D   **A**   **G**   **D/F♯**   **A**

| Oth - er times I can | $\frac{2}{4}$ bare - ly | $\frac{4}{4}$ see. | | |

D   **B**   **F♯**   **B/F♯**   **F♯**

| Late - ly it oc - | $\frac{2}{4}$ curs to | $\frac{4}{4}$ me, | | what a |

                                    w/ riff

A   **E**

| long, | strange trip it's been. | | | | ‖

Chorus

                                           strum chords

E   **A**

| 3. Truck - in' like the | doo - dah man, | once told me you got to |
| 6. Truck - in', I'm a | go - in' home. | Whoa, whoa, ba - by, back where |

                           B

| play your hand. | Some - times the cards ain't | worth a dime, |
| I be - long. | Back home, sit down and | patch my bones and |

                                w/ riff

A   **E**   ***To Coda*** ⊕

| if you don't lay 'em down. | | | | | ‖
| get back truck - in' on. | | | | |

Verse

E

| 3. What in the world ev-er be-came of | sweet Jane? She | lost her spar - kle, you know she is-n't the |

| same. | Liv-in' on Reds, Vit-a-min C and | co - caine, | |

                                                              D.S. al Coda
                                                              (take repeat)

| all a friend can say is ain't it a | shame. | ‖

⊕ **Coda**

Outro-Guitar Solo   ***Repeat and fade***

‖: **E** | | | :‖

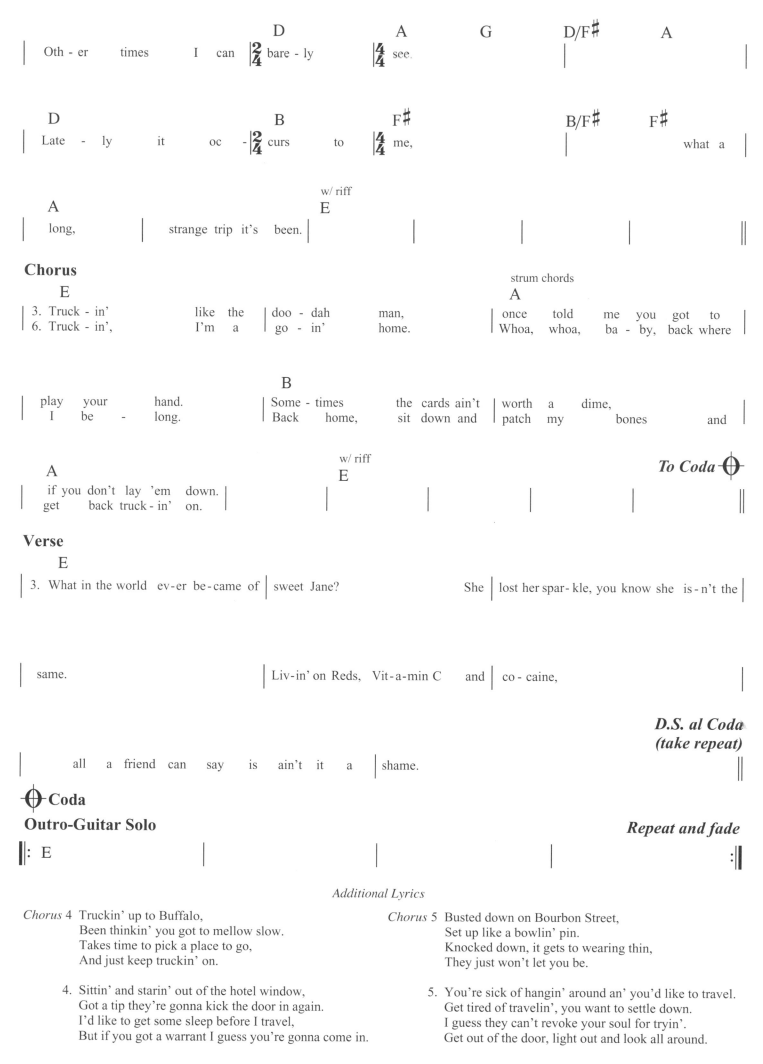

Additional Lyrics

Chorus 4 Truckin' up to Buffalo,
        Been thinkin' you got to mellow slow.
        Takes time to pick a place to go,
        And just keep truckin' on.

    4. Sittin' and starin' out of the hotel window,
        Got a tip they're gonna kick the door in again.
        I'd like to get some sleep before I travel,
        But if you got a warrant I guess you're gonna come in.

Chorus 5 Busted down on Bourbon Street,
        Set up like a bowlin' pin.
        Knocked down, it gets to wearing thin,
        They just won't let you be.

    5. You're sick of hangin' around an' you'd like to travel.
        Get tired of travelin', you want to settle down.
        I guess they can't revoke your soul for tryin'.
        Get out of the door, light out and look all around.

Wagon Wheel

Words and Music by Bob Dylan and Ketch Secor

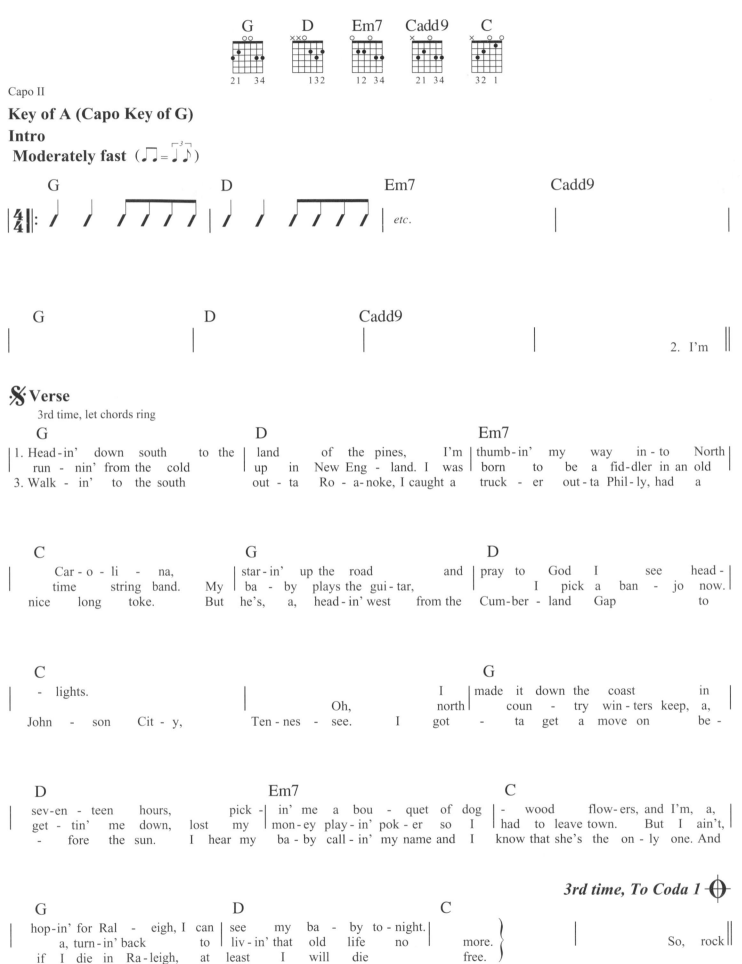

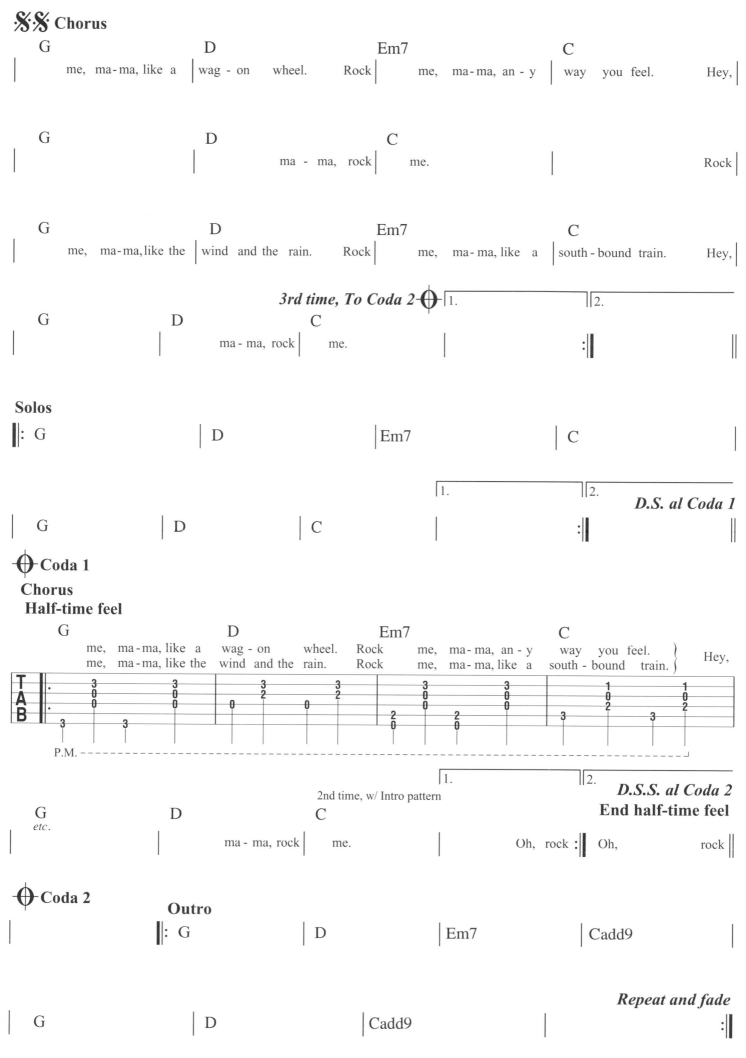

Wake Up Little Susie

Words and Music by Boudleaux Bryant and Felice Bryant

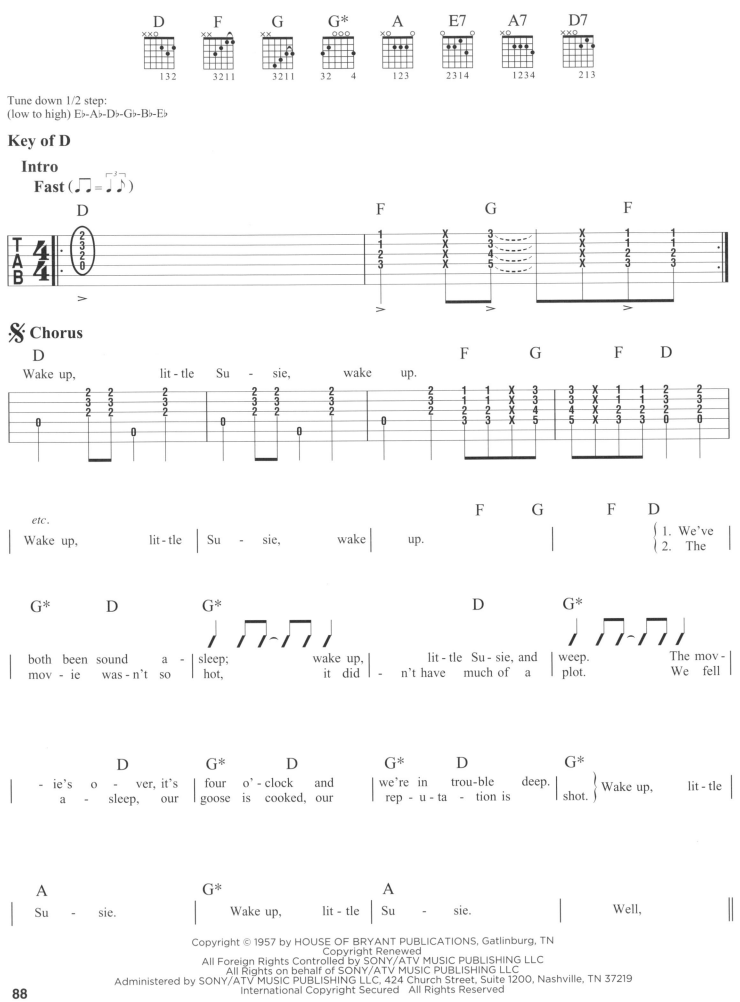

Tune down 1/2 step:
(low to high) E♭-A♭-D♭-G♭-B♭-E♭

Key of D

Verse

A	E7	A		E7	A
what are we gon-na tell your ma	- ma?	What are we gon-na tell your pa?			

	E7	A	N.C.	
What are we gon-na tell our friends	when they say,	"Ooh, la,	la?" Wake up, lit - tle	

To Coda ⊕

D	A7	D	A7
Su - sie.	Wake up, lit - tle Su - sie.		Well, I

Bridge

D		D7
told your ma - ma that you'd be in by ten.	Well,	

G*	
Su - sie, ba - by, looks like we goofed a - gain.	Wake up, lit - tle

A7	G*	A7	N.C.
Su - sie.	Wake up, lit - tle Su - sie.		We got - ta go

D.S. al Coda

D	F G F D	F G F
home.		

⊕ **Coda**

A7	D
Wake up, lit - tle Su - sie.	

Outro

Repeat and fade

‖: D | F G F D | F G F :‖

We Can Work It Out

Words and Music by John Lennon and Paul McCartney

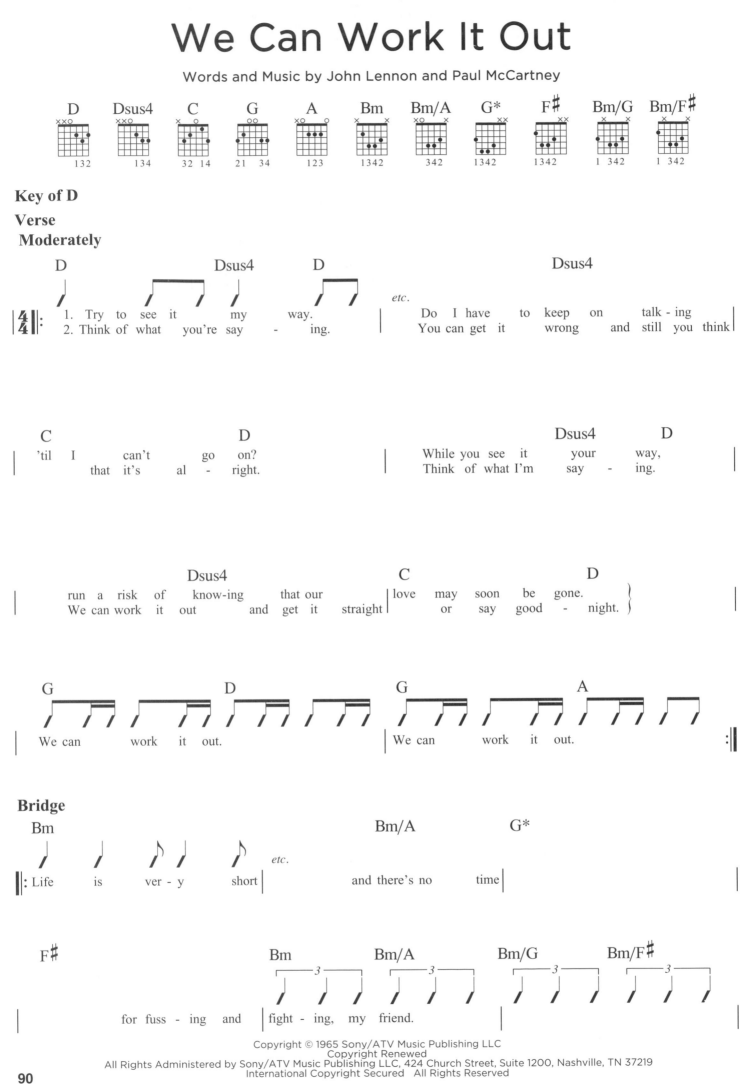

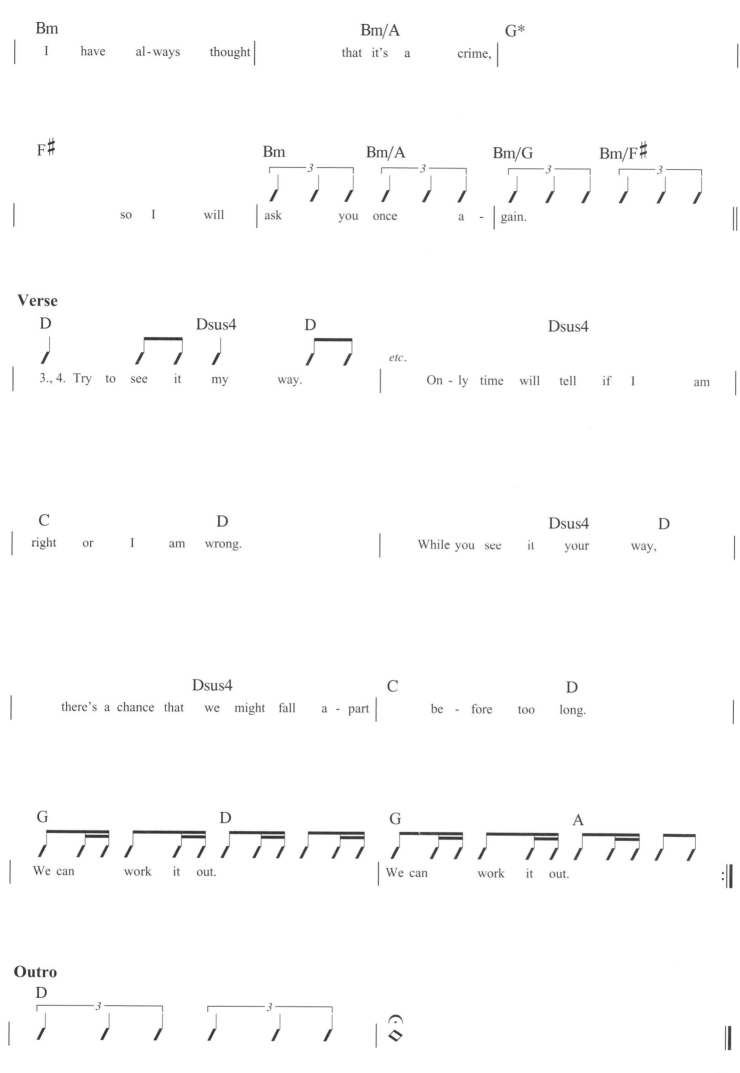

Bm
I have al-ways thought | that it's a crime, |

F#   Bm   Bm/A   Bm/G   Bm/F#
so I will | ask you once a - | gain.

Verse

D   Dsus4   D   Dsus4
3., 4. Try to see it my way. *etc.* On - ly time will tell if I am |

C   D   Dsus4   D
right or I am wrong. While you see it your way, |

Dsus4   C   D
there's a chance that we might fall a - part | be - fore too long. |

G   D   G   A
We can work it out. | We can work it out.

Outro

D

What I Got

Words and Music by Brad Nowell, Eric Wilson, Floyd Gaugh and Lindon Roberts

1.

Interlude

| D5   G5 | D5   G5 | D5   G5 |

2.

Chorus

D5   G5   D5   G5   D5   G5

2. Well, life   :| Lov - in'   is what I   got. | I said re - mem - ber that.

D5   G5   D5   G5   D5   G5

Lov - in'   is what I   got. | and re - mem - ber that. | Lov - in'   is what I   got.

D.S. al Coda

D5   G5   D5   G5   D5   G5

I said re - mem - ber that. | Lov - in'   is what I   got, | I   got,   I   got,   I   got. ‖

Coda

Interlude

*D5   D5   G5   D5   G5

to   me.   ‖

*Let chord ring.

D5   G5   D5   G5   **D5

'Cause ‖

**Let chord ring.

Chorus

D5   G5   D5   G5   D5   G5

lov - in'   is what I   got. | I said re - mem - ber that. | Lov - in'   is what I   got.

D5   G5   D5   G5   D5   G5

and re - mem - ber that. | Lov - in'   is what I   got. | I said re - mem - ber that.

Outro   ***Repeat and fade***

D5   G5   D5   G5   D5   G5   D5   G5

Lov - in'   is what I   got, | I   got,   I   got,   I   got. ‖:   :‖

93

Wild World

Words and Music by Cat Stevens

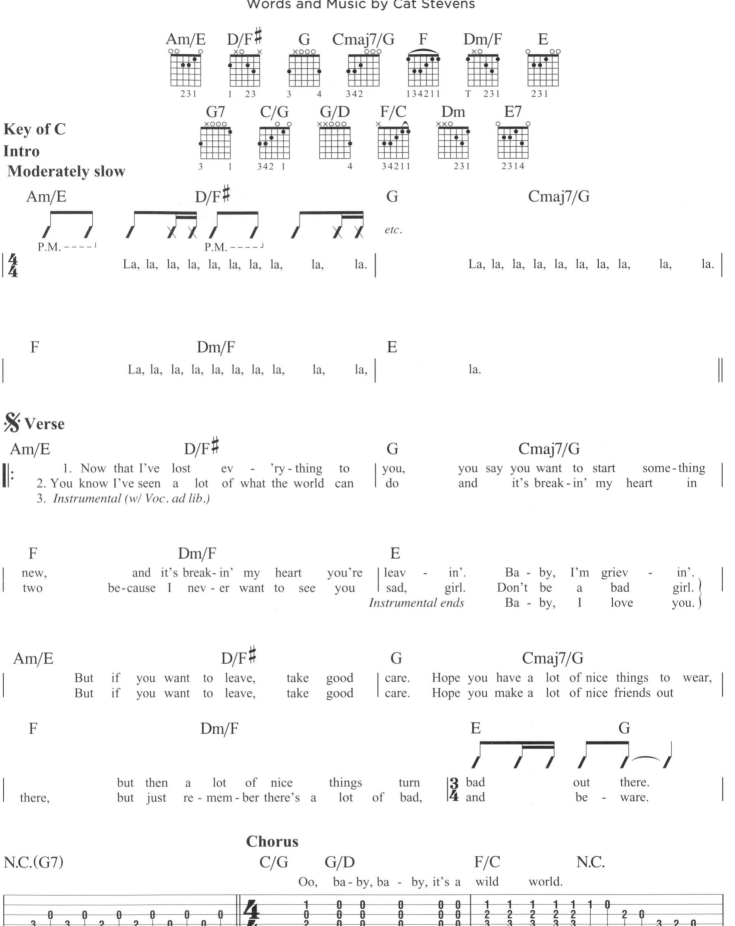

Key of C

Intro

Moderately slow

Am/E — La, la, la, la, la, la, la, la, la, la.
P.M. D/F# P.M. G Cmaj7/G — La, la, la, la, la, la, la, la, la, la.

etc.

F — La, la, la, la, la, la, la, la, la, la, Dm/F E — la.

Verse

Am/E D/F# G Cmaj7/G
1. Now that I've lost ev - 'ry-thing to you, you say you want to start some-thing
2. You know I've seen a lot of what the world can do and it's break-in' my heart in
3. *Instrumental (w/ Voc. ad lib.)*

F Dm/F E
new, and it's break-in' my heart you're leav - in'. Ba - by, I'm griev - in'.
two be-cause I nev-er want to see you sad, girl. Don't be a bad girl.
Instrumental ends Ba - by, I love you.

Am/E D/F# G Cmaj7/G
But if you want to leave, take good care. Hope you have a lot of nice things to wear,
But if you want to leave, take good care. Hope you make a lot of nice friends out

F Dm/F E G
but then a lot of nice things turn 3/4 bad out there.
there, but just re-mem-ber there's a lot of bad, and be - ware.

Chorus

N.C.(G7) C/G G/D F/C N.C.
Oo, ba - by, ba - by, it's a wild world.

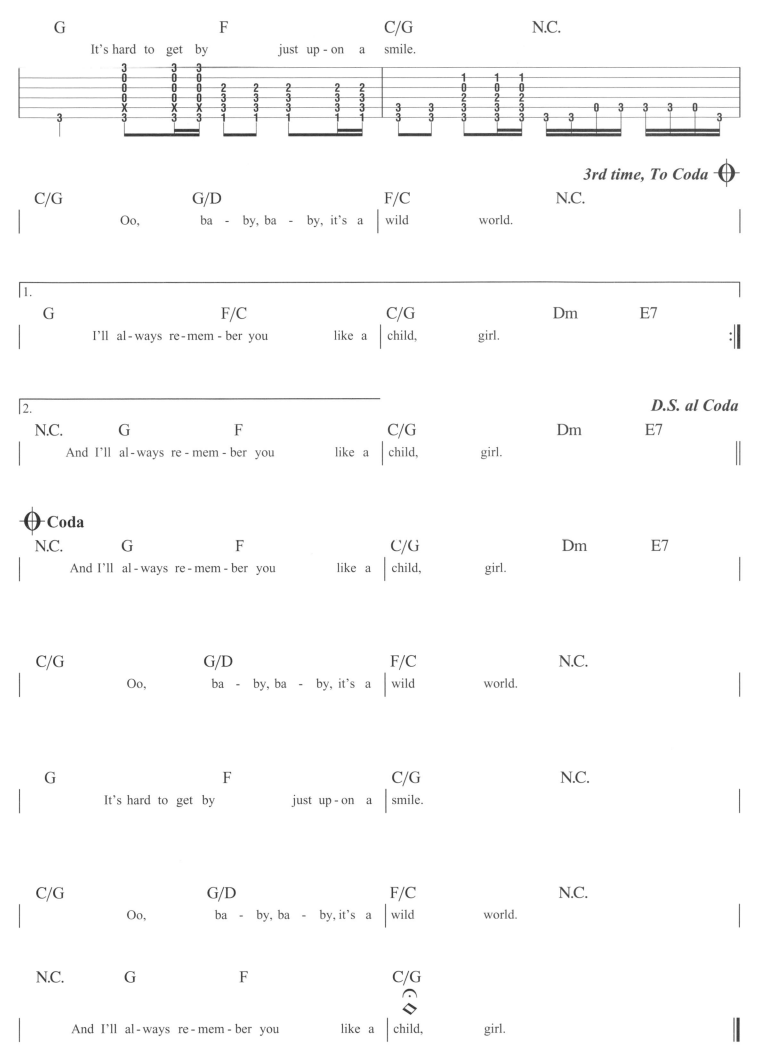

Wish You Were Here

Words and Music by Roger Waters and David Gilmour

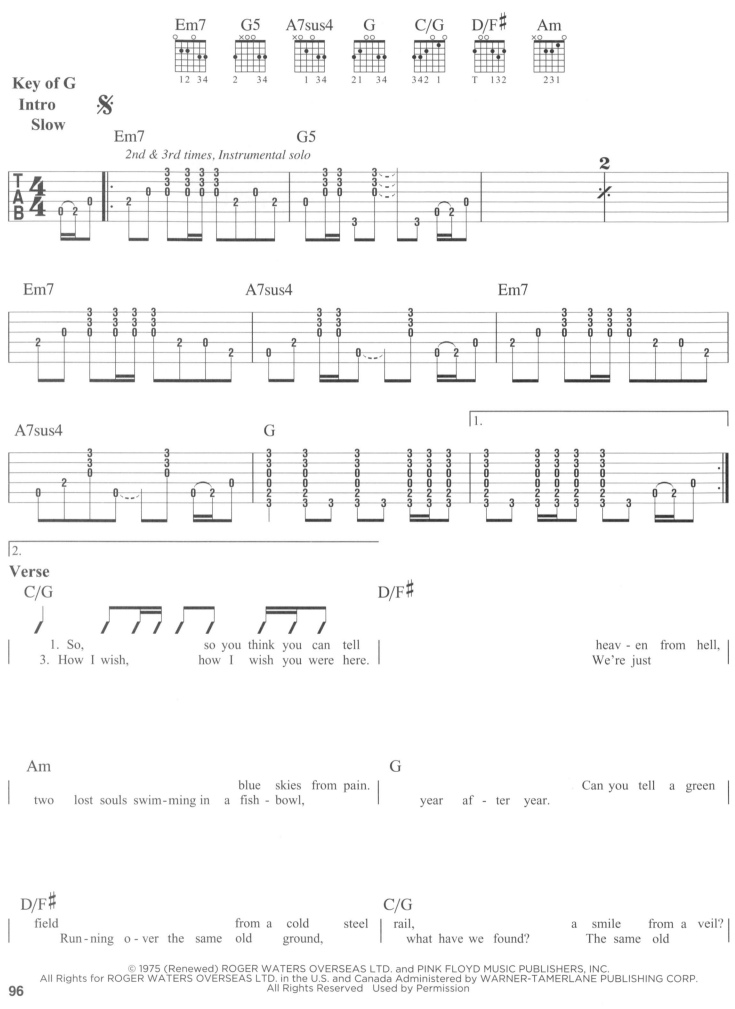

Key of G
Intro
Slow

Verse

1. So, so you think you can tell heav-en from hell, We're just
3. How I wish, how I wish you were here.

two lost souls swim-ming in a fish-bowl, blue skies from pain. Can you tell a green

year af-ter year.

field from a cold steel rail, a smile from a veil?
Run-ning o-ver the same old ground, what have we found? The same old

To Coda ⊕

Am   **G**

| fears,   Do you think you can tell? | 2. Did they get you to trade ‖
        wish you   were here.

Verse

C/G   **D/F♯**

| your he - roes for | ghosts,   hot ash - es for trees, |

Am   **G**

| hot air for a cool | breeze,   cold com-fort for change? |

D/F♯   **C/G**

| Did you ex - change | a walk-on part in the war |

D.S. al Coda
(take 2nd ending)

Am   **G**

| for a lead role in a cage? | ‖

Outro-Guitar Solo

     w/ Intro pattern

‖: Em7 | G5 | Em7 | G5 |

| Em7 | A7sus4 | Em7 |

Repeat and fade

| A7sus4 | G | :‖

Yellow

Words and Music by Guy Berryman, Jon Buckland, Will Champion and Chris Martin

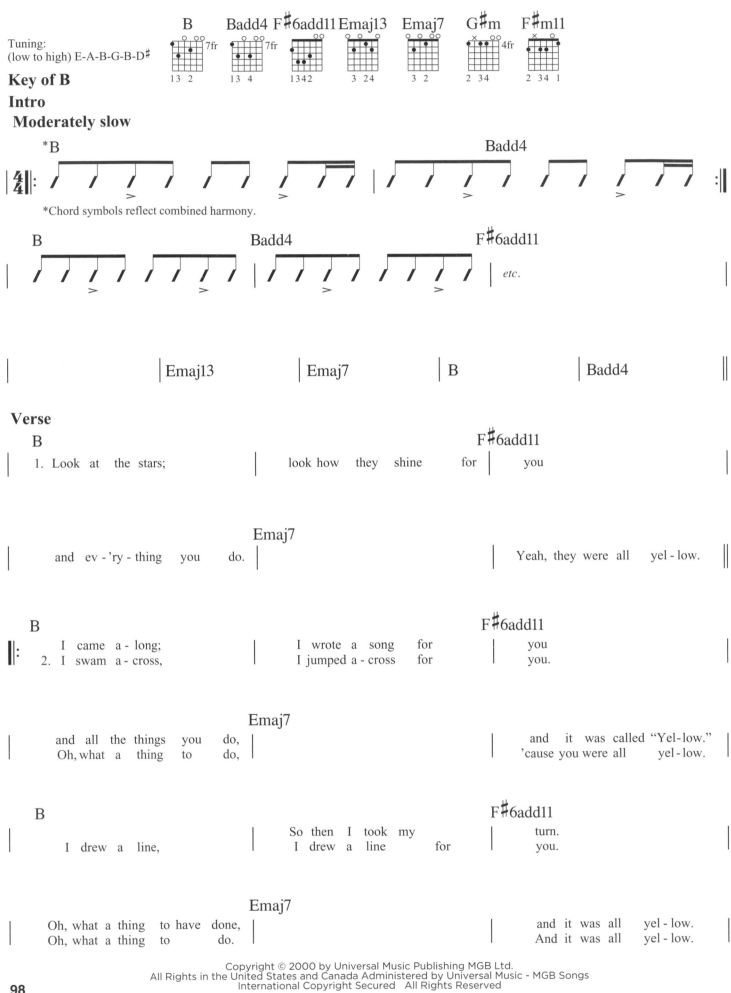

Tuning:
(low to high) E-A-B-G-B-D♯

Key of B

Intro

Moderately slow

*Chord symbols reflect combined harmony.

etc.

Verse

1. Look at the stars; look how they shine for you

and ev-'ry-thing you do. Yeah, they were all yel-low.

I came a-long; I wrote a song for you.
2. I swam a-cross, I jumped a-cross for you.

and all the things you do, and it was called "Yel-low."
Oh, what a thing to do, 'cause you were all yel-low.

I drew a line, So then I took my turn.
I drew a line for you.

Oh, what a thing to have done, and it was all yel-low.
Oh, what a thing to do. And it was all yel-low.

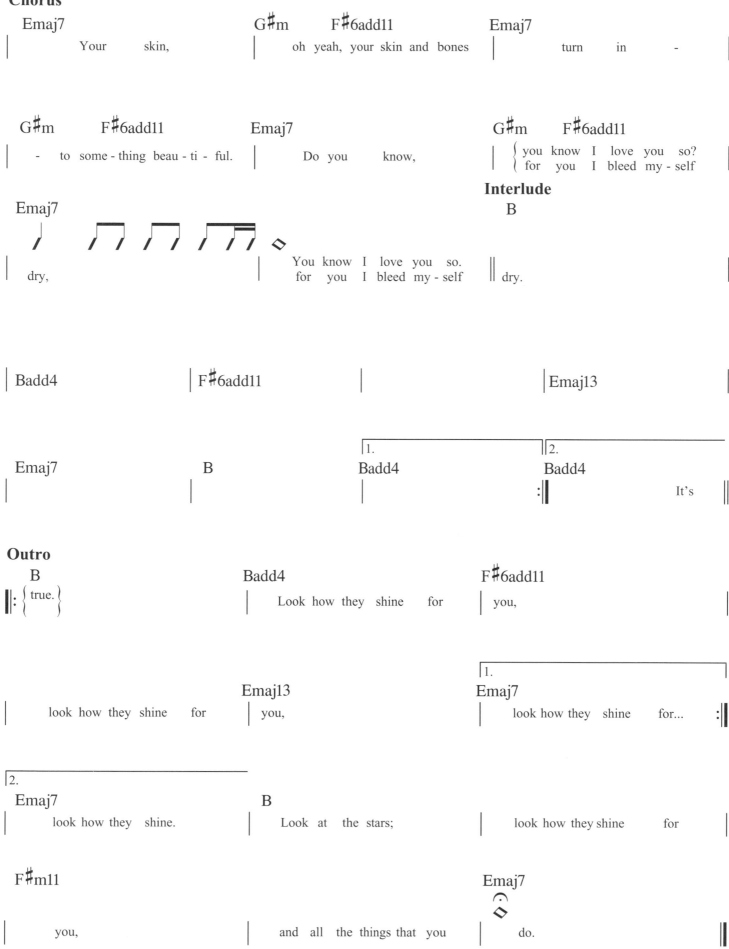

|B| |Badd4   B ||

Chorus

Emaj7   G#m   F#6add11   Emaj7
| Your   skin, | oh yeah, your skin and bones | turn   in - |

G#m   F#6add11   Emaj7   G#m   F#6add11
| - to some - thing beau - ti - ful. | Do you   know, | { you know I love you so? | { for you I bleed my - self

Interlude

Emaj7   B
| dry, | You know I love you so. || dry. |
| | for you I bleed my - self |

|Badd4 |F#6add11 | |Emaj13 |

                                              |1. |2.

Emaj7   B   Badd4   Badd4
| | | :|| It's ||

Outro

B   Badd4   F#6add11
||: { true. } | Look how they shine   for | you, |

                                                               |1.
                     Emaj13   Emaj7
| look how they shine   for | you, | look how they shine   for...   :||

|2.
Emaj7   B
| look how they   shine. | Look at   the   stars; | look how they shine   for |

F#m11   Emaj7
| you, | and all the things that you | do. ||

Yesterday

Words and Music by John Lennon and Paul McCartney

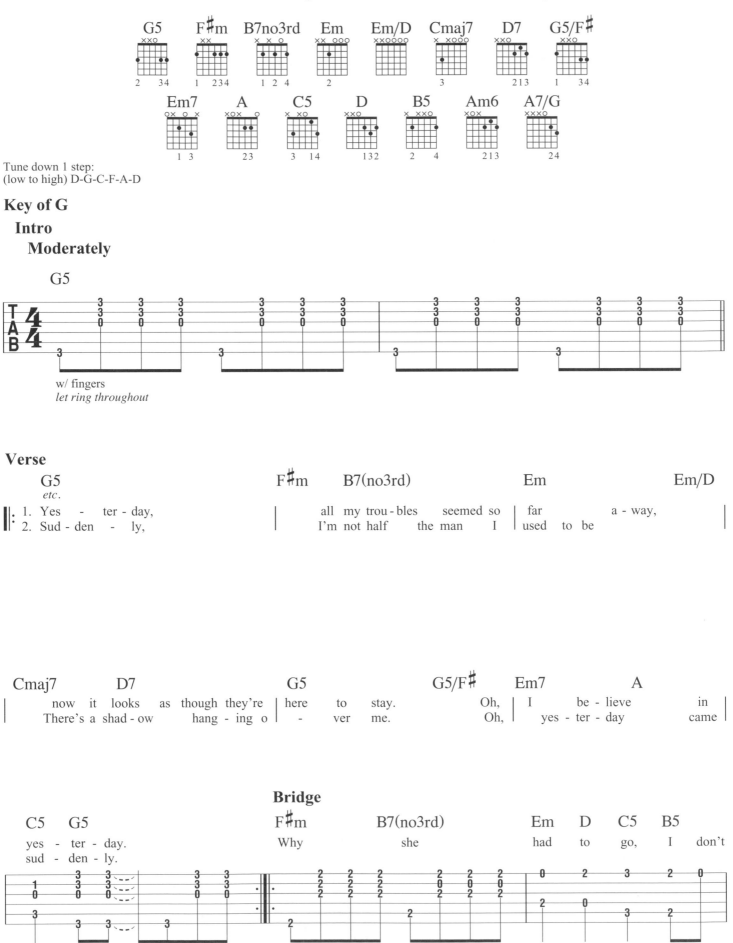

Tune down 1 step:
(low to high) D-G-C-F-A-D

Key of G

Intro

Moderately

Verse

Bridge

Am6			D7		G5		F#m		B7(no3rd)

| know, | she | would - n't | say. | I | said |

Em	D	C5	B5	Am6	D7	G5

| some - thing | wrong, | now | I | long | for | yes - ter - | day. |

Verse

G5	F#m	B7(no3rd)	Em	Em/D

3., 4. Yes - ter - day, love was such an eas - y game to play,

Cmaj7	D7	G5	G5/F#	Em7	A

now I need a place to hide a - way, Oh, I be - lieve in

Outro

C5	G5	G5	A7/G	C5	G5

yes - ter - day. Mm.

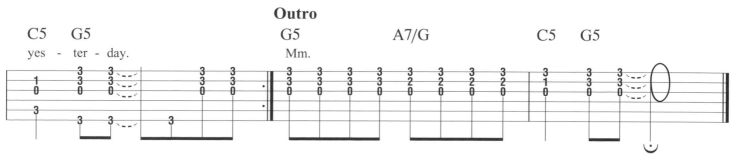

101

RHYTHM TAB LEGEND

Rhythm Tab is a form of notation that adds rhythmic values to the traditional tab staff.

TABLATURE graphically represents the guitar fingerboard. Each horizontal line represents a string, and each number represents a fret. Rhythmic values are shown using ovals, stems, and dots.

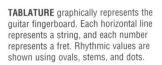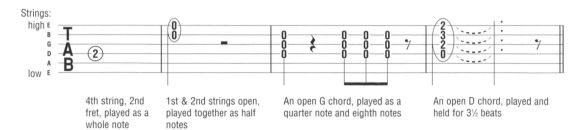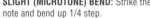

4th string, 2nd fret, played as a whole note

1st & 2nd strings open, played together as half notes

An open G chord, played as a quarter note and eighth notes

An open D chord, played and held for 3½ beats

Definitions for Special Guitar Notation

HALF-STEP BEND: Strike the note and bend up 1/2 step.

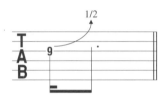

WHOLE-STEP BEND: Strike the note and bend up one step.

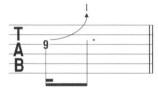

GRACE NOTE BEND: Strike the note and immediately bend up as indicated.

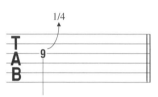

SLIGHT (MICROTONE) BEND: Strike the note and bend up 1/4 step.

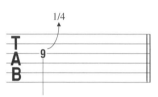

BEND AND RELEASE: Strike the note and bend up as indicated, then release back to the original note. Only the first note is struck.

PRE-BEND: Bend the note as indicated, then strike it.

PRE-BEND AND RELEASE: Bend the note as indicated. Strike it and release the bend back to the original note.

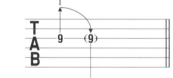

UNISON BEND: Strike the two notes simultaneously and bend the lower note up to the pitch of the higher.

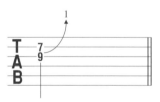

HOLD BEND: While sustaining bent note, strike note on different string.

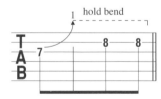

VIBRATO: The string is vibrated by rapidly bending and releasing the note with the fretting hand.

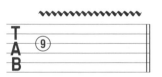

WIDE VIBRATO: The pitch is varied to a greater degree by vibrating with the fretting hand.

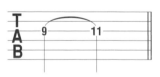

HAMMER-ON: Strike the first (lower) note with one finger, then sound the higher note (on the same string) with another finger by fretting it without picking.

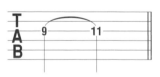

PULL-OFF: Place both fingers on the notes to be sounded. Strike the first note and without picking, pull the finger off to sound the second (lower) note.

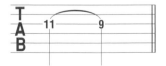

HAMMER FROM NOWHERE: Sound note(s) by hammering with fret hand finger only.

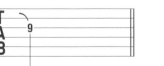

GRACE NOTE SLUR: Strike the note and immediately hammer-on (or pull-off) as indicated.

GRACE NOTE SLUR (CLUSTER): Strike the notes and immediately hammer-on (or pull-off) as indicated.

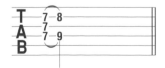

LEGATO SLIDE: Strike the first note and then slide the same fret-hand finger up or down to the second note. The second note is not struck.

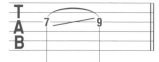

SHIFT SLIDE: Same as legato slide, except the second note is struck.

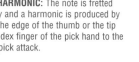

TRILL: Very rapidly alternate between the notes indicated by continuously hammering on and pulling off.

TAPPING: Hammer ("tap") the fret indicated with the pick-hand index or middle finger and pull off to the note fretted by the fret hand.

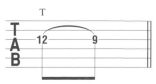

NATURAL HARMONIC: Strike the note while the fret-hand lightly touches the string directly over the fret indicated.

Harm.

PINCH HARMONIC: The note is fretted normally and a harmonic is produced by adding the edge of the thumb or the tip of the index finger of the pick hand to the normal pick attack.

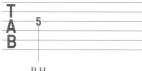

P.H.

HARP HARMONIC: The note is fretted normally and a harmonic is produced by gently resting the pick hand's index finger directly above the indicated fret (in parentheses) while the pick hand's thumb or pick assists by plucking the appropriate string.

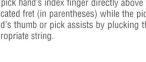

H.H.

PICK SCRAPE: The edge of the pick is rubbed down (or up) the string, producing a scratchy sound.

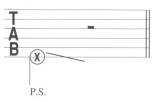

P.S.

MUFFLED STRINGS: A percussive sound is produced by laying the fret hand across the string(s) without depressing, and striking them with the pick hand.

PALM MUTING: The note is partially muted by the pick hand lightly touching the string(s) just before the bridge.

P.M. - - - - - - - - -⌐

RAKE: Drag the pick across the strings indicated with a single motion.

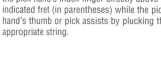

rake - - ⌐

TREMOLO PICKING: The note is picked as rapidly and continuously as possible.

ARPEGGIATE: Play the notes of the chord indicated by quickly rolling them from bottom to top.

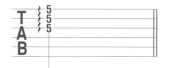

VIBRATO BAR DIVE AND RETURN: The pitch of the note or chord is dropped a specified number of steps (in rhythm), then returned to the original pitch.

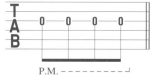

w/ bar -1

VIBRATO BAR SCOOP: Depress the bar just before striking the note, then quickly release the bar.

w/ bar - - - - - - - - ⌐

VIBRATO BAR DIP: Strike the note and then immediately drop a specified number of steps, then release back to the original pitch.

w/ bar - - - - - - ⌐

Additional Musical Definitions

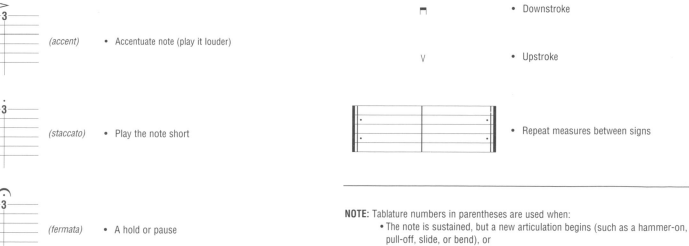

(accent) • Accentuate note (play it louder)

(staccato) • Play the note short

(fermata) • A hold or pause

⊓ • Downstroke

V • Upstroke

• Repeat measures between signs

NOTE: Tablature numbers in parentheses are used when:
• The note is sustained, but a new articulation begins (such as a hammer-on, pull-off, slide, or bend), or
• A bend is released.

FIRST 50

Books in the First 50 series contain easy to intermediate arrangements for must-know songs. Each arrangement is simple and streamlined, yet still captures the essence of the tune.

First 50 Baroque Pieces
You Should Play on Guitar
Includes selections by Johann Sebastian Bach, Robert de Visée, Ernst Gottlieb Baron, Santiago de Murcia, Antonio Vivaldi, Sylvius Leopold Weiss, and more.
00322567...$14.99

First 50 Bluegrass Solos
You Should Play on Guitar
I Am a Man of Constant Sorrow • Long Journey Home • Molly and Tenbrooks • Old Joe Clark • Rocky Top • Salty Dog Blues • and more.
00298574...$16.99

First 50 Blues Songs
You Should Play on Guitar
All Your Love (I Miss Loving) • Bad to the Bone • Born Under a Bad Sign • Dust My Broom • Hoodoo Man Blues • Little Red Rooster • Love Struck Baby • Pride and Joy • Smoking Gun • Still Got the Blues • The Thrill Is Gone • You Shook Me • and more.
00235790...$17.99

First 50 Blues Turnarounds
You Should Play on Guitar
You'll learn cool turnarounds in the styles of these jazz legends: John Lee Hooker, Robert Johnson, Joe Pass, Jimmy Rogers, Hubert Sumlin, Stevie Ray Vaughan, T-Bone Walker, Muddy Waters, and more.
00277469...$14.99

First 50 Chords
You Should Play on Guitar
American Pie • Back in Black • Brown Eyed Girl • Landslide • Let It Be • Riptide • Summer of '69 • Take Me Home, Country Roads • Won't Get Fooled Again • You've Got a Friend • and more.
00300255 Guitar......................................$12.99

First 50 Classical Pieces
You Should Play on Guitar
Includes compositions by J.S. Bach, Augustin Barrios, Matteo Carcassi, Domenico Scarlatti, Fernando Sor, Francisco Tárrega, Robert de Visée, Antonio Vivaldi and many more.
00155414...$16.99

First 50 Folk Songs
You Should Play on Guitar
Amazing Grace • Down by the Riverside • Home on the Range • I've Been Working on the Railroad • Kumbaya • Man of Constant Sorrow • Oh! Susanna • This Little Light of Mine • When the Saints Go Marching In • The Yellow Rose of Texas • and more.
00235868...$16.99

First 50 Guitar Duets
You Should Play
Chopsticks • Clocks • Eleanor Rigby • Game of Thrones Theme • Hallelujah • Linus and Lucy (from *A Charlie Brown Christmas*) • Memory (from *Cats*) • Over the Rainbow (from *The Wizard of Oz*) • Star Wars (Main Theme) • What a Wonderful World • You Raise Me Up • and more.
00319706...$14.99

First 50 Jazz Standards
You Should Play on Guitar
All the Things You Are • Body and Soul • Don't Get Around Much Anymore • Fly Me to the Moon (In Other Words) • The Girl from Ipanema (Garota De Ipanema) • I Got Rhythm • Laura • Misty • Night and Day • Satin Summertime • When I Fall in Love • and more.
00198594 Solo Guitar $16.99

First 50 Kids' Songs
You Should Play on Guitar
Do-Re-Mi • Hakuna Matata • Let It Go • My Favorite Things • Puff the Magic Dragon • Take Me Out to the Ball Game • Won't You Be My Neighbor? (It's a Beautiful Day in the Neighborhood) • and more.
00300500 ....$15.99

First 50 Licks
You Should Play on Guitar
Licks presented include the styles of legendary guitarists like Eric Clapton, Buddy Guy, Jimi Hendrix, B.B. King, Randy Rhoads, Carlos Santana, Stevie Ray Vaughan and many more.
00278875 Book/Online Audio...........$14.99

First 50 Riffs
You Should Play on Guitar
All Right Now • Back in Black • Barracuda • Carry on Wayward Son • Crazy Train • La Grange • Layla • Seven Nation Army • Smoke on the Water • Sunday Bloody Sunday • Sunshine of Your Love • Sweet Home Alabama • Working Man • and more.
00277366...$14.99

First 50 Rock Songs You Should
Play on Electric Guitar
All Along the Watchtower • Beat It • Brown Eyed Girl • Cocaine • Detroit Rock City • Hallelujah • (I Can't Get No) Satisfaction • Oh, Pretty Woman • Pride and Joy • Seven Nation Army • Should I Stay or Should I Go • Smells like Teen Spirit • Smoke on the Water • When I Come Around • You Really Got Me • and more.
00131159...$15.99

First 50 Songs by the Beatles You
Should Play on Guitar
All You Need Is Love • Blackbird • Come Together • Eleanor Rigby • Hey Jude • I Want to Hold Your Hand • Let It Be • Ob-La-Di, Ob-La-Da • She Loves You • Twist and Shout • Yellow Submarine • Yesterday • and more.
00295323...$19.99

First 50 Songs
You Should Fingerpick on Guitar
Annie's Song • Blackbird • The Boxer • Classical Gas • Dust in the Wind • Fire and Rain • Greensleeves • Road Trippin' • Shape of My Heart • Tears in Heaven • Time in a Bottle • Vincent (Starry Starry Night) • and more.
00149269...$16.99

First 50 Songs You Should
Play on 12-String Guitar
California Dreamin' • Closer to the Heart • Free Fallin' • Give a Little Bit • Hotel California • Leaving on a Jet Plane • Life by the Drop • Over the Hills and Far Away • Solsbury Hill • Space Oddity • Wish You Were Here • You Wear It Well • and more.
00287559...$15.99

First 50 Songs You Should Play on
Acoustic Guitar
Against the Wind • Boulevard of Broken Dreams • Champagne Supernova • Every Rose Has Its Thorn • Fast Car • Free Fallin' • Layla • Let Her Go • Mean • One • Ring of Fire • Signs • Stairway to Heaven • Trouble • Wagon Wheel • Yellow • Yesterday • and more.
00131209 ....$16.99

First 50 Songs
You Should Play on Bass
Blister in the Sun • I Got You (I Feel Good) • Livin' on a Prayer • Low Rider • Money • Monkey Wrench • My Generation • Roxanne • Should I Stay or Should I Go • Uptown Funk • What's Going On • With or Without You • Yellow • and more.
00149189 ....$16.99

First 50 Songs
You Should Play on Solo Guitar
Africa • All of Me • Blue Skies • California Dreamin' • Change the World • Crazy • Dream a Little Dream of Me • Every Breath You Take • Hallelujah • Wonderful Tonight • Yesterday • You Raise Me Up • Your Song • and more.
00288843 ....$17.99

First 50 Songs
You Should Strum on Guitar
American Pie • Blowin' in the Wind • Daughter • Hey, Soul Sister • Home • I Will Wait • Losing My Religion • Mrs. Robinson • No Woman No Cry • Peaceful Easy Feeling • Rocky Mountain High • Sweet Caroline • Teardrops on My Guitar • Wonderful Tonight • and more.
00148996 Guitar.....................................$16.99

HAL•LEONARD®
www.halleonard.com

1022
014

Prices, contents and availability subject to change without notice.